More Praise for *The Project Meeting Facilitator*

"Jan, Tammy, and Michael have done it again! Their previous masterwork, *Facilitating the Project Lifecycle*, was a must-have for every project manager. This time their focus is even sharper: a whole book devoted specifically to the facilitator's role—and to the skills and mindset required to execute that role effectively. This book is so loaded with tools, techniques, and templates that even seasoned project managers will keep their copies close at hand."

—Sam Kaner, author, *Facilitator's Guide to Participatory Decision Making*

"Ineffective meetings become a thing of the past when you put the ideas in *The Project Meeting Facilitator* into practice. The authors not only offer a practical guide to every type of meeting in the project life cycle, they also let practitioners know when they have taken a wrong turn."

—William M. Ulrich, president, Tactical Strategy Group, Inc., and author, *Legacy Systems: Transformation Strategies*

"At last—a practical guide to effective facilitation geared exclusively to the unique needs of project managers! Chock-full of easy-to-apply tools and tips, this book affirms that with proper planning and follow-through, project meeting facilitators really can play a critical role in helping teams accelerate time to results. Virtual project teams and those that work face-to-face will benefit equally."

—Nancy Settle-Murphy, president, Guided Insights

"If we had to pay for every hour we spend in meetings, would we say they are worth it? Not usually in my experience. Well-run meetings, however, are worth every penny. This book provides practical tools and, more importantly, some real insight for the reader to evaluate their personal skill set and target areas for improvement."

—Lynn McDonald, president, Greenlight Dynamics, Inc.

"Finally, a book that specifically addresses the unique facilitation skills required in project management meetings. PMs can easily match the different types of project management meetings with the skill levels and processes best suited for what they are trying to accomplish in each."

—Charles Tombazian, director, Global Strategic Planning Avnet, Inc.

"We know facilitators and facilitation help project teams to be more effective and efficient, but who helps the facilitators? Tammy Adams, Jan Means, and Michael Spivey do, and the opportunity to connect to their knowledge and skill through this book is an important one."

—Cameron Fraser, IAF certified professional facilitator and chair, International Association of Facilitators

"Adams, Means, and Spivey have created a very accessible book for project managers and team leaders who want to improve their facilitation skills. There is a lot here for experienced facilitators, too. Having clearly presented the book in an organized format and a conversational tone, the authors demonstrate their own skills in facilitating (or making easy) the process of planning, running, and troubleshooting project meetings. The opening chapter includes a self-assessment of our project meeting facilitator skills—a quick way to help us pay attention to what we already know and what gaps the book can help close. I like the approach of looking at different types of meetings through the life cycle of a project from initiation to closure. This book is a great reference guide to keep dipping back into as we move through the various stages of a project."

—Julia Young, vice president, Facilitate.com

The Project Meeting Facilitator

Facilitation Skills to Make the Most
of Project Meetings

Tammy Adams
Jan Means
Michael S. Spivey

JOSSEY-BASS
A Wiley Imprint
www.josseybass.com

BICENTENNIAL
1807
WILEY
2007
BICENTENNIAL

John Wiley & Sons, Inc.

Published by Jossey-Bass
A Wiley Imprint
989 Market Street, San Francisco, CA 94103-1741   www.josseybass.com

Wiley Bicentennial logo: Richard J. Pacifico

Jossey-Bass books and products are available through most bookstores. To contact Jossey-Bass directly call our Customer Care Department within the U.S. at 800-956-7739, outside the U.S. at 317-572-3986, or fax 317-572-4002.

Jossey-Bass also publishes its books in a variety of electronic formats. Some content that appears in print may not be available in electronic books.

Library of Congress Cataloging-in-Publication Data

Adams, Tammy, 1959–
    The project meeting facilitator: facilitation skills to make the most of project meetings / Tammy Adams, Jan Means, Michael Spivey.
        p. cm.
    Includes bibliographical references and index.
    ISBN-13: 978-0-7879-8706-0 (pbk.)
    1. Project management—Handbooks, manuals, etc.   2. Meetings—Handbooks, manuals, etc.
3. Group facilitation—Handbooks, manuals, etc.
    I. Means, Jan. II. Spivey, Michael, 1969– III. Title.

    HD69.P75A334 2007
    658.4'56—dc22
                                                                        2007017413

    Printed in the United States of America   FIRST EDITION

HB Printing 10 9 8 7 6 5 4 3 2 1

The Jossey-Bass Business and Management Series

Contents

To my husband, Howard, for challenging me to
live, love, learn, and leave a legacy.
—Tammy Adams

To my parents, Harry and Dorothy Means.
May everyone who reads this remember those
who shaped their life and be thankful.
—Jan Means

To my mentors for their wisdom and faith.
To my parents, Gayle and Peggy Spivey, for their love
and constant encouragement,
and
To my sister, Andrea, for her love and support.
—Michael S. Spivey

Introduction

OBVIOUSLY THIS BOOK IS about projects. It says so right in the title—*The Project Meeting Facilitator*. Projects are how work gets done. They can be as grand as building a space shuttle or as small as building a birdhouse. Regardless of the size, they all have objectives, expected outcomes, a defined start and end, a budget, tasks, and assigned resources (even if that's only you). In organizations, projects are the method for bringing the company's vision to fruition. Projects enable change. They are initiated with various goals aimed to improve service, increase profit, reduce waste, enlarge market share, or speed up cycle time. Such ambitious efforts require diligent oversight and coordination to ensure that projects attain their intended objective. That's where the project manager (PM) comes into the picture. The PM is the person responsible for making sure the project gets from here to there successfully with a minimum of unanticipated problems and risks. But projects involve many more roles than just the PM. There may be leads, analysts, customers, technology and quality resources, business experts, management, and a host of others with the knowledge, authority, or expertise necessary to make the project successful.

This brings us to the topic of *meetings*—the third word in the book title. Meetings are a vehicle for exchanging information, confirming progress, creatively developing deliverables or solutions, making decisions, and growing as a team. Unfortunately, we seem to have a dysfunctional relationship with meetings. We need them, but hate them. Sure, we may have too many of them. Recent surveys show that we spend anywhere from 25 to 50 percent of our time in meetings (depending on our role and responsibilities) (PASS Online, n.d.). But ultimately, meetings provide a means for collaborative thinking, discussion, and deliberation that is invaluable in getting project work done. Sad to say, most of the meetings we've attended fall short of their potential.

But wait. The title of this book includes one more word we have yet to mention—*facilitator*. This word holds the key to making project meetings effective. The facilitator is the one who guides the meeting process—making sure everything and everyone is prepared to do their best work, managing the meeting itself, and documenting the meeting outcomes. Through intentionally planning, using facilitative techniques, and managing group dynamics, this person can transform useless meeting time into productive results. This facilitated collaboration helps people work better together to create the outcomes and project deliverables you need in a focused period of time.

But despite the demonstrated value, extended training in human dynamics and facilitation skills are not a standard part of project, quality, or process management training. This is unfortunate. Knowing how to facilitate people toward desired results greatly increases the potential for both project and self-success. So if you are the project manager, team leader, or in an other support role that regularly places you in situations requiring facilitation of groups or teams, *The Project Meeting Facilitator* has been written for you.

Our goal is simple—to help you become a better project meeting facilitator. We will not attempt to teach you how to facilitate. To do so requires watchful coaching and feedback that simply cannot be provided in book form. We will, however, help you look at project meetings with the eyes of a facilitator, and we'll provide collaborative techniques and practical tips we've found useful in our practice. We'll also share new insights into some well-known meeting tools to help you learn how to actually use them to manage your meetings more effectively.

How to Use This Book

This book is intended to be used as a reference manual. Although we've tried to include enough stories to educate and entertain you, it was never our intention that you sit down and read it through from cover to cover. Instead, let your situation and need guide you to the section and chapter that is most relevant to you.

Section One provides the basics around meeting facilitation and tools. Chapter One introduces the role of the project meeting facilitator (PMF). If you're curious about how to determine whether you're the right facilitator for a particular meeting or how your skill set stacks up against core facilitation competencies, you'll want to read this chapter. Chapter Two looks at two foundational meeting concepts—when to hold a meeting (and when not to) and what constitutes a productive meeting. Chapters Three and Four outline facilitation tools and techniques that can be applied to any type of meeting to better prepare, manage momentum, keep discussions focused, clarify communication, get and keep people engaged, and manage those pesky dynamics of working together. You'll want to delve into these sections to find nuggets that will help you see immediate results.

Section Two looks at twenty of the most common project meetings. For each one we've provided stories and helpful tips, along with the following information:

- When it should occur in relation to other project meetings
- The meeting purpose and objectives
- Suggested participants
- Typical inputs required for the meeting
- Expected outputs of the meeting
- Suggested agenda topics
- Do's and don'ts learned from experience
- A troubleshooting guide for those unique situations

To best use this section, we recommend that you go to the Contents and look up the specific meeting you'll be facilitating. Read through the related information and use it to guide your planning efforts. Prior to the meeting, scan through the Troubleshooting Guide to make sure you've incorporated best practices and know what to do if something unexpected comes up.

And if you want to continue to expand your skills and knowledge, Section Three is for you. In it you'll find some of our favorite books and websites, along with a list of organizations that promote continued learning, networking, and growth in the areas of facilitation and project management.

Like you, we love to learn. So please share your lessons learned, meeting insights, questions, and triumphs with us at TheTeam@FacilitatingProjects.com.

The Project Meeting Facilitator

Section I

Project Facilitation Basics

HAVE YOU EVER BEEN INVOLVED in a project that didn't require a meeting? Neither have we. Project meetings provide a forum for exchanging information, coming up with new ideas or alternatives, making decisions, validating work products, or just learning how to work better together. They can occur on a regular basis or on the spur of the moment. They may involve two people or thirty. But regardless, project meetings are intended to achieve results. And most times you, the project manager, are expected to make it happen—whether you've had facilitation experience or not. So in Section One, we'll give you some guidelines, insights, tool, and techniques to help you make any meeting you lead more productive.

Chapter One introduces you to the concept of the project meeting facilitator (PMF). The PMF is responsible for the end-to-end meeting process, including preparation for, facilitation of, and follow-up on the meeting and its deliverables. This chapter provides a checklist for helping you assess whether you're the right person to be the PMF and suggestions on what to do if you're not. Last, it provides some insight on how to assess and improve your facilitation skills.

Chapter Two takes a look at meetings—specifically project meetings—and how to transform them from an unfortunate waste of resources into a productive way of accomplishing work. It explores the topic of when and when not to hold meetings and what a productive meeting looks like. It challenges you to a higher meeting standard—meetings as well-planned, well-managed journeys that engage participants in discussion, debate, and discovery to reach the desired goal.

But like a carpenter, every facilitator needs a set of tools that will aid in artfully transforming both good wood and knots into the desired product. Chapter Three looks at some familiar yet often underutilized tools to plan and manage meeting pace and momentum, keep discussions focused, and aid in mutual understanding. Rather than discussing how to create these common tools, we've focused on how to actually *use them* in meetings to achieve the desired result: an efficient, effective project meeting.

Chapter Four wraps up the section by looking at techniques for keeping people engaged in the meeting process. This involves both getting them prepared to contribute and managing their involvement during the meeting. To accomplish this, we share insights around such topics as effectively eliciting input, keeping participation balanced, and handling difficult situations.

Remember, a meeting without actionable results is simply a waste of valuable resources. So continue to assess and improve your facilitation skills, hold meetings only when necessary, and apply good meeting practices when you do. These steps alone will move your meetings from a waste to a productive use of time.

Chapter 1

What Is a Project Meeting Facilitator?

Coming together is a beginning. Keeping together is progress. Working together is success.

—HENRY FORD

LEADERSHIP. MANAGEMENT. DIRECTION. RESULTS. All of these words evoke images in our minds—positive images of businesses getting things done effectively.

Let's try another word: *meetings*. Now what images come to mind? Tedious? Tiring? Boring? Unproductive? Waste of time? If you can relate to any of these images, then be encouraged. Meetings need not be a waste of precious project resources. They can be the single most effective vehicle for project collaboration—whether they are used to exchange information, confirm progress, creatively develop deliverables or solutions, make decisions, or grow as a team or individual. You just need to know how to transform meetings in your organization from an unessential drain on resources to a vital means of accomplishing project work. How do you do that? Start by adding meeting facilitation skills to your project management inventory.

Profile of a Project Meeting Facilitator

Ever get to a meeting and sit around for the first five minutes trying to figure out who's leading it? As you wait to see who will step up and take the helm, the discomfort can be obvious. Then the project manager shows up. It seems to be an unwritten assumption that project managers know how to manage not only projects but project meetings. Unfortunately, meeting planning, group dynamics, and general facilitation skills are not typically included in the project manager training program. And whether you are a project manager or a project team member, you've probably already recognized the fact that a significant part of your project experience will revolve around meetings.

So what does it mean to facilitate a project meeting? It does not mean directing, dictating outcomes, or getting everyone to see things from your point of view. It is broader than hosting or being an emcee and more involved than just moderating the discussion or monitoring time. The role of the project meeting facilitator (which we'll refer to as the PMF from here on to make reading easier) is about enabling and guiding. Thinking of yourself as a meeting facilitator will help you start to form a new mental image of your role and its associated responsibilities.

What is the role of a PMF? A meeting is often seen as the two-hour event scheduled this coming Tuesday afternoon at 1:00 PM. But a meeting is a process that requires preparation, delivery, and follow-up. And the PMF is responsible for the entire thing. See Figure 1.1 to get insight into the key activities involved in each of the three phases of the meeting process.

As this figure shows, the core responsibilities of a PMF span the scope of the end-to-end meeting process and include

- Establishing and confirming appropriate meeting objectives and desired outcomes
- Translating those meeting objectives into a productive plan for accomplishing them (that is, agenda design)

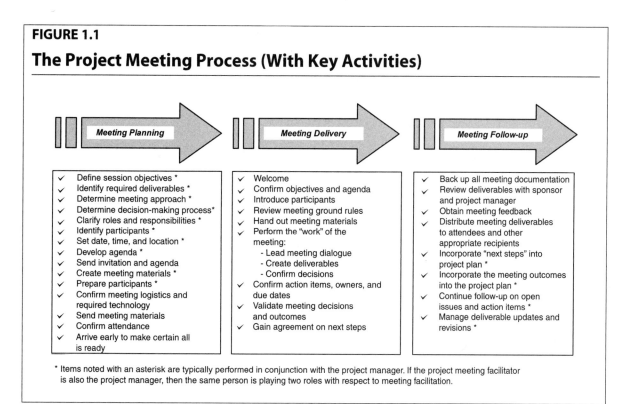

FIGURE 1.1

The Project Meeting Process (With Key Activities)

Meeting Planning

- ✓ Define session objectives *
- ✓ Identify required deliverables *
- ✓ Determine meeting approach *
- ✓ Determine decision-making process*
- ✓ Clarify roles and responsibilities *
- ✓ Identify participants *
- ✓ Set date, time, and location *
- ✓ Develop agenda *
- ✓ Send invitation and agenda
- ✓ Create meeting materials *
- ✓ Prepare participants *
- ✓ Confirm meeting logistics and required technology
- ✓ Send meeting materials
- ✓ Confirm attendance
- ✓ Arrive early to make certain all is ready

Meeting Delivery

- ✓ Welcome
- ✓ Confirm objectives and agenda
- ✓ Introduce participants
- ✓ Review meeting ground rules
- ✓ Hand out meeting materials
- ✓ Perform the "work" of the meeting:
    - Lead meeting dialogue
    - Create deliverables
    - Confirm decisions
- ✓ Confirm action items, owners, and due dates
- ✓ Validate meeting decisions and outcomes
- ✓ Gain agreement on next steps

Meeting Follow-up

- ✓ Back up all meeting documentation
- ✓ Review deliverables with sponsor and project manager
- ✓ Obtain meeting feedback
- ✓ Distribute meeting deliverables to attendees and other appropriate recipients
- ✓ Incorporate "next steps" into project plan *
- ✓ Incorporate the meeting outcomes into the project plan *
- ✓ Continue follow-up on open issues and action items *
- ✓ Manage deliverable updates and revisions *

* Items noted with an asterisk are typically performed in conjunction with the project manager. If the project meeting facilitator is also the project manager, then the same person is playing two roles with respect to meeting facilitation.

- Communicating effectively prior to the meeting to encourage participant readiness

- Ensuring that the right people are in attendance to accomplish the objectives

- Creating an environment that encourages full participation of meeting attendees

- Getting people engaged and participating productively during the meeting to achieve meeting objectives

- Communicating meeting results and incorporating meeting outcomes and next steps to maintain project momentum

- Obtaining and incorporating meeting feedback to continually improve the meeting process

These eight responsibilities describe the role of a PMF, and your ability to carry them out will lay the groundwork for meeting success. We'll give you some tips for improving your skills in these areas in subsequent chapters, but for now start thinking about the change this may require in your typical meeting scheduling and behavior. An effective PMF does not just show up at the meeting start time, out of breath from running between meetings. The PMF doesn't jump ship during the meeting when the going gets tough, or leave outcomes hanging after the meeting concludes. Instead, this person is in the room ahead of time, prepared to lead and guide the team in getting work done. And after the meeting, the PMF follows up effectively to ensure that outcomes are fully documented and used.

Are You the Right Facilitator for the Meeting?

All meetings are not the same; not only do they have different objectives, expectations, and deliverables, but they also vary in tone and complexity. Accordingly, you should not expect to be an effective facilitator for every sort of meeting. We each have meetings that we're more comfortable with based on our individual experiences and preferences. A meeting to facilitate senior management through project strategy and funding decisions is certainly different from a weekly team meeting to confirm project progress. And although you might be a master at status meetings, you may not be the best person to facilitate requirements development meetings. Understanding your personal strengths, preferences, and growth areas will help you determine which meetings best fit your current skills. Table 1.1 shows a range of meeting situations and the recommended level of skill needed for each.

You may ask: how do I assess my skill level? Let's look at three levels of facilitation ability: novice, skilled, and expert. As a general rule, *novice facilitators* are those who are fairly new to facilitation. They understand the basic mechanics of scheduling and agendas, but have little experience with or training in group dynamics or more advanced facilitation techniques.

Skilled facilitators have solid meeting capabilities and the competence to confidently lead when confronted with roadblocks or unexpected issues. They have probably received some

---

TABLE 1.1

Matching Facilitation Skills to Meeting Needs

Meeting Type	Recommended Facilitation Skill Level	What Is Required of the Facilitator
Information exchange	Novice to skilled	Sharing of information is typically a more straightforward meeting situation. Often this type of meeting presents fewer challenges regarding the dynamics of the group. Even in this less volatile meeting type, facilitators must be able to remain poised in front of the group. They must be able to present and exchange information clearly, checking for understanding throughout the process. This type of meeting can be useful for mentoring new facilitators and bringing their skills to a level where they are confident to face more challenging meeting situations.
Creative development	Skilled to expert	Meetings requiring creative development generally mean that ideas are being generated and challenged, with the result often being the creation of specific project deliverables. These may range from simple to complex in content, but the dynamic of the group in these situations generally calls for a facilitator with strong skills.
Decision making	Skilled to expert	Meetings requiring decision making can be difficult in both content and human dynamics. Facilitators must be able to maintain their composure in difficult situations, defuse conflict, and encourage participation. The ability to lead a group through healthy debate, option identification, and challenges and into final decisioning (to confirm project direction or finalize project deliverables) requires strong facilitation skills.
Coaching	Expert	Meetings that provide feedback and coaching to team members call for an expert level of facilitation skill. This requires the ability to identify areas of strength and challenge and to give instruction in the recommended steps for growth without alienating or discouraging the team members.

sort of facilitation training or have grown through years of lessons learned the hard way. They use many of the meeting tools and techniques described in Chapters Three and Four, and they are generally perceived as good meeting managers.

You'd be considered an *expert facilitator* if, in addition to your advanced skill in facilitation, you possess specialized knowledge or experience (or both) in such fields as coaching, psychology, team development, or quality processes and tools. Your ability to apply this specialized knowledge to your group facilitation gives you additional tools for handling difficult audiences and situations and complex objectives.

Although Table 1.1 provides some general guidance, you'll need to carefully consider other aspects of your meeting situations, such as complexity of subject matter, management hierarchy, political nature of the participants, and the potential for meeting volatility, as you determine whether the meeting fits your facilitation abilities.

It is also important to consider whether the meeting participants will accept you in the role of PMF. Often it's hard for folks to separate their role as project manager from their role as meeting facilitator. Have you had previous experience with any of the participants such that your credibility as a facilitator may be questioned? If so, consider the impact this may have on meeting objectives and outcomes. If it is significant, then we suggest that you select another facilitator—one whom the group will be able to view as objective in the role as meeting facilitator. This role clarity can be tough—both for you and for the team. We watched one project manager ask her team for input, wait approximately two seconds, and then tell them what she believed to be the right answer. She was obviously struggling with the concept of directing versus facilitating. In this case, meeting results were never owned by the team, and her future credibility as a meeting facilitator was damaged.

So are you the right facilitator for the meeting? It's been said that you never get a second chance to make a first impression. And when people have a bad meeting experience, they are less likely to actively participate in future gatherings. This loss of collaboration can potentially jeopardize project success. Weigh

---

EXHIBIT 1.1

Can I Facilitate This Meeting?

As you're preparing for your next meeting, ask yourself these questions to make sure you're the right person for the job:

Will the group be able to view me as unbiased and objective?

Can I use my knowledge and expertise to ask questions that guide the group rather than giving answers or dictating solutions?

Do I understand the expected outcomes of the meeting, and will I be able to lead the group to deliver these?

Do I feel comfortable handling the dynamics and politics of the meeting?

Does this meeting require any specialized analysis, modeling, or facilitation techniques, and if so, will I be able to apply these techniques with the group?

---

the cost and be sure you have the capabilities necessary to handle the meeting requirements.

Throughout this conversation, you may be asking yourself the question, "If not me, then who?" You may not have the luxury of getting someone else to act as the meeting facilitator. In those cases, we'd recommend that you do one of the following:

- Identify someone whom you consider an expert in meeting facilitation and ask that person for coaching in how to address your specific meeting situation.

- Invite one or two of the meeting attendees to assist during the meeting by supporting you in capturing information, meeting decisions, or action items, so that you can concentrate more fully on managing the group dynamics and meeting agenda.

- Practice the meeting in your head. Athletes use this visualization technique consistently prior to competition. They see the situation, think through the activities, and mentally practice the movements to formulate the experience of winning in their head prior to the actual event. Do this as a meeting facilitator. Think through the meeting. What is the best-case scenario? What is the worst-case scenario? What could go awry? What contingency plans should you have ready if things do not go as you planned?

These recommendations will not automatically transform you into the right facilitator for every meeting, but they will increase your level of success in difficult meeting situations.

Assessing Your Skill Level

Whether you are just beginning in facilitation or you've done it for years, it is beneficial to periodically take a step back to assess your progress and capabilities. Facilitation is neither a science nor completely an art. And there is no cookie-cutter approach to being consistently successful at facilitation. Success lies in the facilitator's ability to creatively apply skills in each group setting to accomplish the objectives at hand. So does that mean facilitation skills and competencies are indefinable? Absolutely not. The International Association of Facilitators (IAF) has developed a set of six core competencies by which to assess your facilitation skills (Pierce, Cheesebrow, and Mathews Braun, 2000). We've augmented that list with nine additional skills identified by our clients over the years as critical in meeting facilitation (see Exhibit 1.2).

Use this list as a tool to assess your strengths and challenges, get a baseline of your current abilities, and create a plan for improvement. First assess yourself, then ask one or more of your project colleagues to assess you with the same questionnaire. Incorporate this feedback into your improvement plan and revisit the assessment in thirty days to evaluate your growth. Mastering these competencies will give you a comprehensive foundation for successful facilitation. Your application of these competencies in meeting situations will determine your success.

Applying Your Skills

It is important to recognize that the nature of facilitation requires that we embrace what may often seem to be contradictions.

EXHIBIT 1.2

Project Meeting Facilitator Self-Assessment

Please respond to the following competencies according to the level of confidence you have in your ability to demonstrate these when facilitating project meetings.

Facilitator Competency	1 Low	2	3 Med	4	5 High
1. Ability to create collaborative client relationships					
a. Developing working partnerships with the meeting sponsor and participants					
b. Designing and customizing meetings and work sessions to meet client needs					
c. Managing multisession events effectively					
2. Ability to plan appropriate group processes					
a. Selecting clear methods and processes that will achieve the desired meeting outcome					
b. Preparing time and place to support group process					
3. Ability to create and sustain a participatory environment					
a. Demonstrating effective participatory and interpersonal communications skills					
b. Honoring and recognizing diversity, ensuring inclusiveness within the meeting					
c. Managing group conflict					
d. Evoking group creativity					
4. Ability to guide groups to appropriate and useful outcomes					
a. Guiding the group with clear methods and processes					
b. Facilitating group self-awareness about its task					
c. Guiding the group to consensus and desired outcomes					
5. Ability to build and maintain professional knowledge					
a. Maintaining a base of knowledge about facilitation					
b. Knowing a range of facilitation methods and techniques					
6. Ability to model positive professional attitudes					
a. Practicing self-assessment and self-awareness					
b. Acting with integrity					
c. Trusting group potential and modeling neutrality					
7. Demonstrating general communication skills					
a. Listening actively					
b. Questioning effectively					
c. Observing					
d. Confirming meaning					
e. Summarizing					
f. Validating					

EXHIBIT 1.2 *(continued)*

Facilitator Competency	1 Low	2	3 Med	4	5 High
8. Demonstrating group communication skills					
a. Balancing participation					
b. Encouraging creativity					
c. Managing conflict					
d. Supporting the group process					
e. Maintaining neutrality while challenging the group					
9. Demonstrating analytical skills					
a. Reasoning inductively					
b. Reasoning deductively					
c. Gathering pertinent information					
d. Synthesizing information					
e. Problem solving					
10. Demonstrating conceptual skills					
a. Generating ideas					
b. Building connections					
c. Linking concepts					
11. Demonstrating technical skills					
a. Building appropriate deliverables, using the appropriate techniques					
b. Generating models					
c. Ensuring consistency and correctness					
d. Applying appropriate modeling rules and conventions					
12. Demonstrating leadership skills					
a. Motivating					
b. Encouraging consensus					
c. Managing expectations					
d. Fostering an environment of trust					
e. Facilitating decision making					
13. Demonstrating political awareness					
a. Exhibiting tact					
b. Being diplomatic					
c. Navigating the organizational hierarchy					
d. Recognizing the formal and informal organization					

EXHIBIT 1.2

Facilitator Competency	1 Low	2	3 Med	4	5 High
14. Demonstrating management skills					
a. Organizing					
b. Delegating					
c. Planning					
d. Following through					
15. Demonstrating presentation skills					
a. Speaking clearly					
b. Using appropriate terminology					
c. Writing legibly					
d. Being aware of body language					
e. Engaging the right presentation technology for the situation					
f. Knowing your audience					

Overall, I would describe my facilitator competencies as _____

In the next two weeks, I will work on improving _____

- You must step up to the challenge of being a process leader while at the same time being a servant to the needs of the group.

- You must demonstrate expertise in guiding a group effectively through a set of tasks to meet objectives, yet be flexible enough to try alternate routes if you encounter obstacles or a substantive reason to change direction.

- You must probe for clarity and insight, yet remain neutral to the content provided. This kind of neutrality does not mean being ambivalent about results; rather, it is the ability to question the group, listen for understanding, and challenge group thinking rather than providing the answers yourself. You must be comfortable with letting others find the answers.

- You must be focused both on accomplishing the task and on managing and growing the people.

- You must understand yourself—your preferences and biases—while being keenly aware of the preferences and biases of those in your meeting group.
- You must be able to manage group dialogue while pulling out significant points to synthesize, confirm the meaning, and interpret into the correct deliverable content.
- You must be engaged with the group "in the moment," yet thinking ahead to what is coming next.

How do you balance these seemingly conflicting elements? By viewing the world through three different lenses at any given moment—the lenses of process, people, and self (Means and Adams, 2005).

Keep an eye on the process. This process orientation means that you're paying attention to what's happening in the meeting—ensuring that the activities achieve the desired objectives and result in value-added products.

Stay aware of the people involved. Having a people orientation means that you engage people with active listening and questioning. You synthesize and integrate their responses, challenge ideas, get feedback, and clarify results. You also manage how people work together effectively throughout the meeting process: in planning, delivering the work session, and executing follow-up activities.

Remain aware of yourself. This self-awareness involves being conscious of your own strengths and weaknesses, preferences and biases, and being able to use or control these as appropriate to lead the work session participants in meeting their objectives.

Keeping in mind these three orientations—process, people, and self—during a meeting will help you maintain balance amid the myriad of seeming contradictions. Remember, it's not just the gathering of knowledge but also application through diligent practice that enables skills to develop. And as a project manager you'll get plenty of opportunities to practice. So try new techniques, improve your observation of yourself and others, and mature in your competence by repeated practice and feedback.

Summing It Up

- Growing and developing good PMFs in your organization is one of the key building blocks to revitalizing meetings. It aids in changing the perception from "meetings are a waste of time" to "meetings are essential to getting the buy-in and focused time needed to get the work done." Well-managed and -executed meetings are necessary for project success.

- To be effective, the PMF must be more than a meeting host or emcee. The PMF is engaged in and responsible for all aspects of meeting preparation, delivery, and follow-up.

- Just as all meetings are not created equal, neither are meeting facilitators. If you want the meeting to be successful, make sure you have the level of skill necessary to achieve the desired outcome.

- Remember that it is important for the group to ascribe credibility to the facilitator. Has the selected facilitator had previous experience with any of the participants such that his or her credibility as a facilitator may be questioned? If so, consider the impact this may have on meeting objectives and outcomes. If it is significant, then select another facilitator—one whom the group will be able to accept and trust in the role as meeting facilitator.

- Whether you are just beginning in meeting facilitation or consider yourself a pro, remember that it is always wise to assess your strengths and challenges on a periodic basis. Engage in self-assessment and request feedback from other respected colleagues. The resulting insights will benefit your professional and personal growth.

- Meetings are a triple-juggling act—managing the process, the people, and yourself—and to be successful, you must keep all three balls moving without dropping them.

Chapter 2
The Basics of Project Meeting Facilitation

> It must not be supposed that the conference table
> possesses the magic property of generating wisdom
> when rubbed simultaneously by a dozen pairs of elbows.
> —WILLIAM E. UTTERBACK

THE MERRIAM-WEBSTER DICTIONARY defines the term *meeting* as "an act or process of coming together" (Merriam-Webster Online Dictionary, 2007). Often this is the extent to which project managers think about meetings—they forget that the definition is merely a description rather than a result. Project management is based on the principle of collaboration—"the act of working together with one or more people in order to achieve something" (Encarta World English Dictionary, 2006). For project managers, you can translate the phrase "working together" as meetings and "to achieve something" as getting desired results. By extending the simple concept of meetings to include working together and getting desired results, you can improve project management considerably. Imagine how your mind-set toward meetings would change if, every time you attended one, the team worked together and achieved results! Yet few project managers focus on these things. Instead, they mistakenly assume that improving their team's ability to work together and walking out with tangible results are simply by-products of coming together.

Meetings—whether by phone, videoconference, face-to-face, or some creative combination—provide a way for teams to exchange information, raise awareness, grow in knowledge or skills, perform creative or critical thinking, get validation, come to agreement, improve morale, accomplish tasks, and much more (Duncan, 1999). All of these are critical to the success of a project and its project manager. The success of meetings employs both art and skill, starting with knowing when and when not to meet.

When to Meet—and When Not to Meet

Meetings are often viewed as time wasters, unfortunately with good reason. A 2004 survey commissioned by Interactive Meeting Solutions (2004b) found that

- 55% of meetings are dominated by one or two people.
- 32% of people feel they could get fired for speaking the truth in a meeting.
- 39% of decisions are made once the meeting is over.
- 80% of the discussion is about things people already agree on.

Obviously, some of these meetings should have never been held. But could the PMF have realized that ahead of time? We think

How Do You Feel About Meetings?

According to a random telephone survey of 1,216 American workers conducted by Interactive Meeting Solutions, almost a third of the country's workforce (29 percent) now attends three or more meetings a week—and 40 percent of American workers say many of those meetings are a "complete waste of time."

so. Let's walk through a few guidelines to help you evaluate whether a project meeting will be beneficial rather than an unfortunate waste of resources. You should hold a meeting only if the following are true:

- The reason for the meeting is essential to the project.
- The goal requires collaborative interaction.
- The right people can be present.
- There's someone to manage the meeting process.

We'll present guidelines for each of these and explore the reasoning behind them. We will also give you some options for avoiding the status quo by using good facilitative practices.

The Reason for the Meeting Is Essential to the Project

Don't let tradition (we've always done it this way) or methodology (you have to do this because it's part of our quality or project process) dictate the need for a meeting. Have you experienced this nightmare? You're drowning in a sea of unnecessary meetings, paperwork, and deliverables, doing everything you can to simply keep your head above water, shouting at those above you to throw some resources your way or adjust the unrealistic deadlines. But instead, they just keep lobbing you those clichéd

---

Meeting "Must-Haves"

Do not hold a meeting without having defined and communicated its
1. Purpose
2. Desired outcome(s)
3. Duration
4. Location, link, or dial-in number
5. Basic agenda
6. Mandatory participants
7. Necessary prework, if any

cement life preservers of "we'll just have to make it work" or "it'll all come together" while you go under for the last time.

Make sure there's a reason—a real need—for the meeting. In one of "Bryce's Laws," author Tim Bryce states: "Unless someone is looking for an excuse to duck a work assignment, nobody wants to attend an inconsequential meeting" (Bryce, 2006). We've all sat through more of these than we'd like to remember. In one case, a project sponsor spent two days talking *at* the team—providing them with information and asking nothing in return. In another, the meeting was framed as "brainstorming," but turned out to be an exercise to validate what the executive had already decided. Project team members have enough to do without the added burden of attending unnecessary meetings. So before you hold a meeting, spend some time thinking through your meeting purpose and desired outcomes. Then communicate these to your team in a way that stresses their value in the process.

Have a Clear Purpose and Outcome

You should have a documented purpose and desired outcomes for each meeting you lead. In fact, don't attend meetings that lack these elements! The purpose statement communicates why the meeting is being held. The outcome describes what tangible results you want to attain. It allows team members to assess their value to the meeting in light of competing priorities and come better prepared to achieve the outcome. So ask yourself, "What are the objectives that must be accomplished?" And make sure they relate to the expectations of the meeting only, not to the project as a whole (Means and Adams, 2005). See Table 2.1 for an illustration of some sample meeting purposes and corresponding outcomes.

Communicate WIIFM

Let's face it—most of us are driven by self-interest. Every time we're asked to join, be involved, or take action, we instinctively

TABLE 2.1

Examples of the Difference Between a Meeting Purpose and Its Desired Outcomes

Meeting Purpose	Desired Outcomes
To get clarity on issues affecting the project	• Clear definition of the issues and their impacts • Recommendation or decision (depending on the impact) about how to handle the issues • A high-level estimate of what the resolution will cost in terms of resource hours, money, and downstream delays
To establish the project timeline and interdependencies	• Definition of a realistic end-to-end timeline of project milestones and activities • An understanding of which activities may be potential constraints • Identification of any issues needing to be addressed to validate or change the timeline
To kick off the project	• An understanding of project charter, high-level scope, and timeline by all attendees • Confirmation of project meeting schedule • Identification of any concerns regarding the charter, scope, or timeline as presented
To provide project overview or status to management	• An understanding of the project and its current progress and high-impact issues by all attending managers • Validation or approval of direction on high-impact issues • Identification of any outstanding concerns • Confirmation of next steps
To review change controls for the project	• A clear understanding of the need for the change • An understanding of how the change will affect other concurrent and downstream activities • Identification of any previously undiscussed concerns regarding the change

evaluate "What's in it for me?" (WIIFM). That's not a bad thing. If a topic is relevant or intriguing or somehow impacts us, we're more likely to pay attention. So communicate your meeting goals in a way that helps participants see how they can contribute to the meeting and what they'll gain from it.

The Intel Corporation has done a great job of incorporating this philosophy into practice. "You can walk into any conference room at any Intel factory or office anywhere in the world and you will see a poster on the wall with a series of simple questions about the meetings that take place there: *Do you know the purpose of this meeting? Do you have an agenda? Do you know your role?*" (Matson, 1996). Understanding their role—the value their specific expertise brings to the meeting—allows participants to evaluate relative priorities and make better decisions about attendance. If you can't articulate a meeting purpose that enables the participants to understand how they add value, then you may be inviting the wrong participants or you may need to rethink the purpose of your meeting.

The Goal Requires Collaborative Interaction

How many project status calls have you attended where everyone stays muted (and continues working, instant messaging each other, or holding off-line conversations) until they hear their name or project mentioned? Countless hours have been spent on these calls with limited value. True, some issues have been raised. But has the cost to the whole really been worth the value gained? We don't think so.

Many project activities require the involvement of others—in thinking, doing, validating, or approving. The key is to know how much you can do *without* holding a meeting. Here are our general guidelines for making this determination:

- *Do it yourself and communicate it* when you are the decision maker, are aware of the impacts, and are willing to be accountable for the consequences. As a project manager, you may decide to create and communicate the project meeting schedule or the project status reporting format rather than holding a meeting to discuss it.

- *Draft it and have it reviewed* when you are not the decision maker but have broad insight into the topic and its impacts.

Bring the draft to the meeting as a starting point to get the team thinking. But remember to give the team the freedom and authority to adjust the draft as needed to represent their shared vision and understanding.

- *Get others involved* when you don't have the broad subject matter expertise required to create a draft, in which case the necessity of holding a meeting will be based on whether you need just one person or a group of people to provide the knowledge necessary to accomplish the goal.

Fortunately, with the advent of blogs, wiki's, and other collaborative technologies, project teams now have alternative methods for gathering routine information. Many of our clients have created project websites for large-scale efforts to store documents, post the latest status, and allow blogging of issues. Bottom line: ask yourself if there's any other way to communicate or receive the needed information *before* you decide to hold a meeting to do it.

The Right People Can Be Present

Just common sense, right? Yet something's not working. In an informal survey of project managers performed by Resource Alliance in 2006, 32 percent of the respondents indicated that incorrect or inadequate meeting attendance was the primary cause of meeting ineffectiveness (Resource Alliance, 2006).

In an attempt to get the "right" people in the meeting, some organizations have implemented the buckshot approach—send your meeting notice to the widest possible audience, and you're bound to get someone. This approach requires little assessment of meeting needs and ensures that you don't miss anyone, but it produces some unfortunate results. Your meeting notice may be ignored or overlooked in the deluge (especially if this is a common practice in the organization). The people who do show up may not be the ones capable or appropriate to achieve the meeting goal. So in the end you get less than you hoped for and expend the same amount of time and energy doing it.

Instead, consider a more focused approach to getting the right people in your meeting. Identify the four to six people who are mandatory to achieving your goal. Take into account the topics you'll be discussing, the level of detail you need to delve into, and the length of the meeting (two hours versus two days) to make sure the people you have in mind are suitable. Then invite them by framing the meeting purpose in terms that are relevant and important to them. Ask them to either confirm that they are the right people or recommend someone who is. This type of focused approach requires early communication to avoid calendar conflicts and is best accompanied by a communication from the project sponsor indicating the meeting's importance in light of other organizational priorities.

If, after all your efforts, you can't get the people you need when you need them, consider alternate meeting attendance options such as these:

- Allow key participants to attend only the portion of the meeting where their area of expertise is most needed. This requires some extra meeting planning when crafting the agenda. It also requires additional meeting management to ensure that comments and issues arising at other times during the meeting are captured for discussion at the appropriate time.

- Hold a quasi-virtual meeting—some folks face-to-face, others on the phone. This allows key team members to participate even when traveling.

- Gather specialty insight prior to the meeting. Use your wiki, blog, template, or asynchronous meeting software to allow folks to provide input to meeting topics by a set deadline, at which time those who are available will meet.

- Have "on-call" participants. On-call means that you have their cell phone number or pager number or access to them via instant messaging during your meeting and that they will respond to your inquiry promptly. This is especially helpful when you have participants who would be needed only if issues arise in their area of expertise (for example, compliance, security, finance).

There's Someone to Manage the Meeting Process

In the same survey of project managers cited earlier, a lack of effective meeting controls was identified as the primary cause of meeting ineffectiveness by almost half of the respondents (Resource Alliance, 2006) (see Figure 2.1). This lack of controls included allowing participants to go off on tangents, multitask during the meeting, have side conversations, arrive late, and dominate meeting conversations. We'll discuss some techniques for handling many of these issues in Chapters Three and Four, but in the meantime we'll simply say that the responsibility for managing these distractions falls squarely on the shoulders of the project meeting facilitator (whether that is the project manager or someone else). This person must have the necessary facilitation skills and experience to deal effectively with the distractions and keep the meeting focused (see Chapter One for more insight into desired facilitation competencies).

So what do you do if a meeting is necessary, but there's no one who can effectively facilitate it? There are several options.

FIGURE 2.1

Causes of Meeting Ineffectiveness

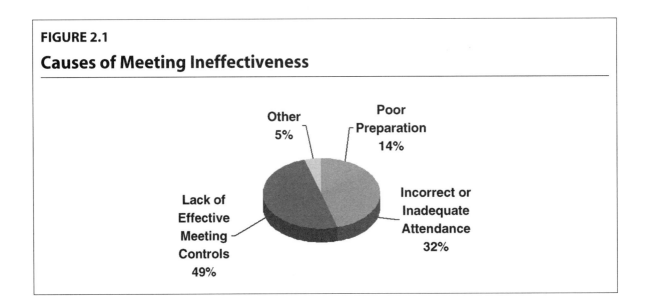

Perhaps you've been in a meeting with someone who seems to be skilled. Request that person's assistance to ensure you attain your desired results. If that's not possible, consider looking outside your department or division. The quality or training departments or even the project/program management offices (PMOs) may have someone sufficiently trained in meeting facilitation techniques. As a third alternative, you may want to hire a facilitation professional—especially if the meeting is high visibility or high risk. See Section Three for resources you can tap into.

Profile of a Productive Meeting

Assuming you've read through all the previous material and decided that a meeting is indeed required, what would a good project meeting look like? What qualities would it have? What are we envisioning when we think of a productive meeting? Simply put, a productive meeting is a well-planned, well-managed journey that engages participants through discussion, debate, or discovery and achieves its intended goal—a goal that is essential to the project, of course.

Project Meeting Characteristics

But how do we get there? By creating a meeting environment that inspires collaboration. That environment, according to Carol Daly in *The Collaboration Handbook* (Daly, 2006), should incorporate the following ingredients in order to be most effective. (We've thrown in a few [*bracketed*] thoughts of our own to tie these concepts more tightly to project meetings.)

- The [*meeting*] process is open, inclusive, transparent, accessible, and tailored to local [*or specific project*] needs.
- Meetings are civil and safe. No bullies allowed. [*No clarification needed here!*]
- Deliberations are thoughtful, frank, and never rushed. [*At the very least, we make sure enough time is scheduled on the*

agenda to gather opinions, when appropriate, and allow thoughtful consideration of those opinions.]

- There is an agreed-upon way to make decisions. [*It can be different for each meeting, but the decision-making process is known to all.*]
- Commitments that are made are honored. Trust is built on that confidence. [*This includes commitments to meeting attendance, ending a meeting at the time promised, and completing agreed-upon tasks.*]
- It's a team effort. You win, you lose, you temporize as a team. [*Projects aren't an individual thing. All members are interdependent for success.*]

Now that's a productive meeting!

Types of Project Meetings

Your profile of a productive meeting would not be complete without understanding the various types of project meetings you'll encounter. We didn't just pick these types at random. After extensive research of meeting types across different professions, we synthesized the results and used our experience to apply them to project meetings. The result was four basic types of (or reasons for) project meetings: information exchange, creative development, decision making, and coaching (see Table 2.2).

Let's take a moment to define each type and look at the related project meetings. Understanding the type of meeting you're shooting for will better help you define its purpose, structure, and outcome. Chapters Five through Nine will go into more detail about the meeting types—giving you insight into objectives, participants, and agendas, and facilitation tips to help you get the results you want.

Information Exchange Meetings

These meetings are held for the purpose of acquiring or disseminating information or both. They can be participative in nature,

TABLE 2.2

Types of Meetings

Type or Purpose	Project Meeting Examples	Nonproject Meeting Examples
Information exchange	• Project kickoff meetings • Project status meetings • Stakeholder review meetings • Executive overview meetings • Project wrap-up meetings	• Sales meetings • Product launches • Depositions • Focus groups • Public feedback forums
Creative development	• Ideation meetings • Strategy meetings • Project scope meetings • Project planning meetings • Key deliverable planning meetings • Key deliverable meetings • Timeline creation meetings • Lessons learned meetings • Risk identification meetings • Crisis resolution meetings • Project retrospective meetings	• Discussion groups • Task forces • Contract negotiations • Management planning retreats
Decision making	• Project charter concurrence meetings • Rules of engagement meetings • Change control review meetings • Project turnover meetings	• Board of directors meetings • Homeowner association meetings • Church committee meetings
Coaching	• Team development meetings • Individual development meetings	• Sales training • Team-building events • AA meetings • Personal trainings

with Q&A or learning application activities, but the intention is for the audience to learn or understand something it previously did not, and the content is not up for debate or change. Examples include

- Project kickoff meetings
- Project status meetings
- Any other report, status, progress, start-up, orientation, announcement, or presentation-type meetings

See Table 2.2 for a list of similar types of project meetings.

Creative Development Meetings

These meetings are held to allow thoughtful discussion and debate about, and input into, a problem, situation, or project deliverable. The result of these meetings will typically be a draft, recommendation, or set of alternatives accompanied by many follow-up tasks to get further insight or input. There may be multiple meetings of this type prior to any sort of review or validation (in a decision-making meeting). Examples of this type include

- Ideation meetings
- Strategy meetings
- Project planning meetings
- Risk identification meetings
- Crisis resolution meetings
- Any other brainstorming, creation, mapping, problem-solving, or investigative meeting

Decision-Making Meetings

These meetings are intended to review, analyze, and ultimately validate or make a decision about something. Typically, a draft, recommendation, or possible scenario has already been created, and time will be spent reviewing and revising it to produce an agreed-upon result. Many project meetings will have a creative development type of meeting first, followed by this type to finalize the output or outcome. Examples include

- Project charter concurrence meetings
- Rules of engagement meetings
- Change control meetings
- Project turnover meetings
- Any other approval, authorization, review, validation, or draft finalization type of meeting

Coaching Meetings

This type of meeting is directional, intended to provide guidance, motivation, coaching, or training to those involved, with the desired result of changing their actions or thinking. Often approached one-on-one, these meetings get folks aligned or re-aligned with project priorities. Examples include

- Team development meetings
- Individual development meetings
- Any training or development meetings

Project Meeting Structure

Within each type, the meetings can range from formal to informal, depending on the nature and complexity of their objectives. They can also vary in frequency—from regularly recurring to specialty, one-time meetings. Both of these elements affect the level of planning, the skill of delivery, and the nature of follow-up needed for the meeting. We'll be addressing these elements in detail for each meeting we discuss in Section Two, but for now let's look at the general implications.

Meeting Formality

Informal meetings are typically smaller in attendance, more ad hoc, and require little formal structure. Their objective is focused, limited to one topic, decision, or issue. Facilitation of informal meetings is less demanding, but don't take that to mean the PMF's task is unnecessary or easy. The everyday work and decisions happen in informal project meetings, so meeting management techniques for keeping on topic and clarifying communication become even more critical. More will be said about these in Chapters Three and Four.

Formal meetings may have multiple objectives requiring a large, diverse set of participants. They require more planning and a more structured agenda. They may even require specialized quality tools or modeling techniques. Because of this, you may want to consider hiring a professional facilitator for these types of meetings.

Meeting Frequency

Some of your project meetings will be recurring, meaning they will be repeated multiple times throughout the project lifecycle. For these meetings, you'll be able to set a regular meeting schedule and use a somewhat standard agenda each time. Some examples include project planning meetings, project status meetings, and even change control meetings. Preparation, delivery, and follow-up for these meetings become normal, repeatable parts of your project management function.

Then there are the specialty meetings—one-time meetings that occur during the project. No matter how many projects you've been involved in, this type of meeting is different every time. Examples include the project charter concurrence meeting, project kickoff, and project retrospective. Some components of the agenda may be standard, but each of these meetings will need specialized thought and preparation to ensure that the needs of that specific team and project are met. You may choose to engage more skilled facilitators to run these events, and follow-up will be more political and visible.

Summing It Up

- Project meetings are intended to produce results—a combination of coming together, working together, and achieving something.
- Hold a meeting only if it is essential to the project, it requires collaborative interaction, you can get the right people to attend, and there's someone to manage the meeting process. If you hold the meeting in the absence of any of these elements, it will create more stress than it will relieve.

- Shoot for productive meetings—well-planned, well-managed journeys that engage participants through discussion, debate, and discovery and achieve their intended goal. Wouldn't that be a change from the status quo—and boost your reputation immensely?

- To help you craft your purpose and objectives, think about the basic type and structure of your meeting. Is it primarily intended to exchange information, creatively come up with something, make a decision or validate something, or encourage growth? Is it a one-time event or will it be repeated? See Chapters Five through Nine for specific insights about each meeting type.

Chapter 3

Facilitation Tools for Keeping Meetings on Target

> The aim of argument, or of discussion, should not be victory, but progress.
> —JOSEPH JOUBERT, French essayist and moralist
> (1754–1824)

THERE ARE SOME BASIC TOOLS every project meeting facilitator should have in his or her tool bag to help meetings flow smoothly. Most of these tools you've seen used—both effectively and ineffectively—in meetings throughout your career. Mentally rewind to some of those experiences. Remember the meeting whose agenda was briefly stated and forgotten? What was the point? And what about those ground rules? It took thirty minutes to get agreement on them, and they weren't even relevant to the work at hand. Then there are all those tasks that folks agreed to do after the meeting. Whatever happened to them? They were discussed, maybe even noted somehow, but never mentioned again. This experience certainly does not coincide with our definition of effective meetings.

We know you're already familiar with the basics of meeting management, but have you ever been told how to actually *use* those meeting tools to focus and manage your meeting? That's our goal. We have no desire to reiterate old knowledge or give you the ideal plan; rather, we want to concentrate on how the tools you're already familiar with can be used to plan and manage meeting pace and momentum, keep discussions focused, and aid in mutual understanding. Thus we will not be describing the how-to's for each tool—there are many books on such topics available in the market (see Section Three, Resource A, for some of our favorites). Instead, we'll focus on how to use these tools to achieve the desired result: an efficient, effective project meeting.

Tools for Meeting Preparation

Dwight D. Eisenhower once said, "In preparing for battle I have always found that plans are useless, but planning is indispensable." This represents the best advice to date on keeping your project meetings on target: prepare. Don't worry about having the perfect plan; it'll change. Instead, be thoughtfully prepared for your upcoming meeting by taking the time to plan.

Meeting planning is a short phrase that encompasses a lot of background work, discussion, and thinking. Figure 3.1 gives you just a glimpse of what the planning stage can involve.

FIGURE 3.1

Meeting Preparation Road Map

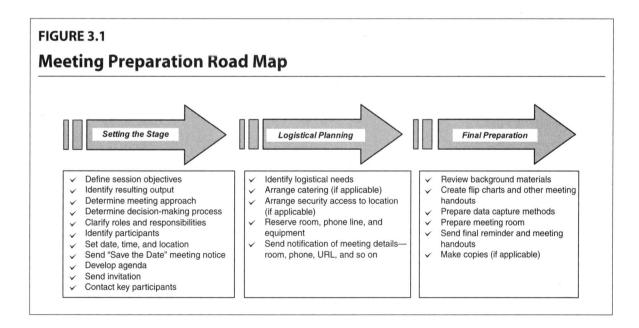

Setting the Stage	Logistical Planning	Final Preparation
✓ Define session objectives ✓ Identify resulting output ✓ Determine meeting approach ✓ Determine decision-making process ✓ Clarify roles and responsibilities ✓ Identify participants ✓ Set date, time, and location ✓ Send "Save the Date" meeting notice ✓ Develop agenda ✓ Send invitation ✓ Contact key participants	✓ Identify logistical needs ✓ Arrange catering (if applicable) ✓ Arrange security access to location (if applicable) ✓ Reserve room, phone line, and equipment ✓ Send notification of meeting details—room, phone, URL, and so on	✓ Review background materials ✓ Create flip charts and other meeting handouts ✓ Prepare data capture methods ✓ Prepare meeting room ✓ Send final reminder and meeting handouts ✓ Make copies (if applicable)

We're not going to spend time delving into all the details around planning. You've heard many of them before. Instead, let's look at a couple of simple tools that will help you make sure you've covered all the bases—the Facilitated Meeting Planning Guide for Project Managers and the Meeting Preparation Checklist.

The Facilitated Meeting Planning Guide for Project Managers

After facilitating meetings for several years, we realized that it would be much easier if we created a repeatable process to guide our steps. No more forgetting little details or overlooking key planning steps. The result was the Facilitated Meeting Planning Guide for Project Managers. This guide assumes that your project has been funded and that a facilitated meeting has already been approved by the project sponsor. It also assumes that someone other than you is playing the role of meeting facilitator. If that is not the case, then you will also need to pay attention to those tasks listed for the facilitator. See the website for a copy of the Facilitated Meeting Planning Guide.

The Meeting Preparation Checklist

The Meeting Preparation Checklist is used in the first step of the Facilitated Meeting Planning Guide. It provides a basic list of considerations around the who, what, when, where, why, and how of the meeting (see Exhibit 3.1).

The checklist is designed for specialty meetings—those with a unique format that may occur only once or infrequently. But if the meeting is repetitive, consider the following during preparation:

- By what date and time will we need updated information for each meeting cycle?
- How will this updated information be gathered?

EXHIBIT 3.1

Meeting Preparation Checklist

☐ Why

- ○ Why are we having the meeting?
- ○ What is the meeting purpose?

☐ What

- ○ What are the objectives that must be accomplished?
- ○ What will be delivered as a result of the meeting?
- ○ What materials need to be brought into the meeting?
- ○ What materials must be reviewed prior to the meeting?

☐ Who

- ○ Who will facilitate the meeting?
- ○ Who needs to contribute before the meeting?
- ○ Who needs to contribute at the meeting?
- ○ Who will handle meeting logistics and setup?
- ○ Who may need to remain involved after the meeting is over to ensure action items are complete and results are communicated?
- ○ Who is making sure that meeting results get communicated and outstanding action items are tracked?

☐ When

- ○ When does the meeting need to take place?
- ○ When are the deliverables going to be used?
- ○ How long does the meeting need to be?
- ○ Will this meeting be repeated? If yes,
  - How often do we need this meeting?
  - Can we establish a standard day, time, objectives, and agenda for the meeting?

☐ How

- ○ How should the agenda be structured to accomplish the objectives?
- ○ What facilitation tools, techniques, or models will be used?
- ○ How will the group make their decisions (consensus, majority rules, other)?
- ○ How will we communicate with participants and other parties before and after the meeting (email, telephone, in person)?

☐ Where

- ○ How should the meeting be accomplished to best meet the objectives (face-to-face or virtual)?
- ○ Will a conference room or rooms be needed?
- ○ What technology is required to support the meeting?
- ○ Will food or other amenities be required?
- ○ Have we communicated all instructions to the participants so that they can join and productively participate in the meeting?

- How will we distribute the current agenda and meeting materials?
- Have the meeting cycle and all repeating preparation activities been communicated to all parties?
- Do we really need to convene the meeting this cycle? This is a seldom asked but very valuable question. Why hold a meeting simply for the tradition of it? If you do decide to cancel, make sure to do so in an adequate amount of time to allow folks to make alternate plans.

See the website for a more complete Meeting Preparation Checklist.

Tools for Managing Momentum and Focus

You're driving through city traffic, with its typical ebbs and flows, trying to reach your destination by a specified time. The first three miles pass quickly. Then you get stuck in traffic. It's start and stop, slow, and tedious, but gradually the flow evens out and you're on your way again. Or so you thought—until an accident up ahead brings things to a screeching halt.

The pace of meetings can be similar. They start off smoothly, as planned, then slowly start to snowball out of control. You just get folks herded back on track when—bam!—you're blindsided with an unexpected comment, issue, or behavior that leaves you wondering if you'll ever achieve your goals. If you've ever had this experience, you'll be pleased to know there are tools to help you minimize those starts and stops and handle those unexpected obstacles.

Just Wait

Give the team a tool for self-managing meeting progress by including the WAIT Principle in your ground rules. The WAIT Principle challenges all participants to take ten to fifteen seconds to ask themselves "**W**hy **A**m **I T**alking?" before jumping into the conversation. By asking that question, they can make sure their comments are relevant to the current topic before opening their mouths. All they have to do is WAIT.

Meeting Purpose and Outcomes

Have you heard the old adage "If you aim at nothing, you'll be sure to hit it"? Many meetings aspire to this goal. Meeting facilitators walk into the room with a vague notion of what they want to achieve and little or no idea of how they will actually make it happen. As a result, they get exactly what they planned for—a statement of desire and little or no tangible progress. That's similar to getting behind the wheel of a car with a vague idea of where you're going and no reason for going there! No wonder such meetings are viewed as a big waste of time.

As mentioned in Chapter Two, every meeting should have a *statement of purpose* accompanied by one or more desired outcomes. A purpose statement is one sentence describing why people are being asked to spend their time in this meeting. The *outcomes* or *objectives* are the tangible results you want to attain. That said, how do you use these elements to manage momentum and focus?

- Use the purpose and outcomes as assessment tools for questionable discussions. You may not always know whether a conversation is relevant to the topic at hand or just a distraction. When you're unsure, ask the team, "Would you help me to understand how this conversation will aid in achieving the desired outcomes?" This simple question refocuses their attention on the goal and allows them to assess the value of continuing discussion.

- Use the purpose and outcomes as a beacon to guide the team. If your meetings are anything like ours, people can get so involved in discussions they forget what they are there to achieve. And although participation is good, walking out of the meeting without results is not. So, like a beacon on a foggy night, periodically remind folks why they are there and what they're shooting for to keep them on target. You might say something like "Remember, we're here to get clarity on what caused yesterday's system outage. So by the time we leave today we need to have a clear understanding of what caused it and what was affected and a plan to prevent it from happening in the future."

Write It Down

If the group keeps going off on tangents, ask them to take a moment and write down their top three ideas around the topic. According to Michael LeBoeuf, author of *Working Smart: How to Accomplish More in Half the Time*, "when you write down your ideas you automatically focus your full attention on them. Few if any of us can write one thought and think another at the same time."

Source: LeBoeuf, 1980, p. 68.

Agenda

Using our previous driving analogy, your agenda is the road map for getting you and your passengers to the destination. Just as driving directions ensure that you arrive at the intended location, a well-thought-out agenda ensures you achieve your objectives. And yet a survey of 150 corporate meetings across fifty industries found that half had no written meeting agenda (Ross, 2006) (see Exhibit 3.2 for other findings). What's wrong with this picture?

Unfortunately, agendas are often viewed as straitjackets rather than aids. Like a map, an agenda is simply a tool to provide you and your participants with some direction and a means to get somewhere (your purpose and objectives). We are

---

EXHIBIT 3.2

Survey of Meeting Practices

Survey Says

A survey of 150 corporate meetings across fifty industries found that

- Half had no written meeting agenda.

- Less than one-third of the observed meetings had someone capturing minutes of the meeting.

- Only one in ten meetings included the critical follow-through process and clear communication of next steps.

Source: Ross, 2006.

reminded of a project manager who sat in the back of the room and waved her arms, pointing to her watch if we spent one minute more than intended on an agenda topic. She mistakenly thought the purpose of the agenda was to manage time rather than to guide the team through the discussion and decisions necessary to achieve the goal (which may result in adjustments to the agenda).

So how can we use this tool to manage momentum and focus?

- Walk through the agenda to bring the team in synch about what they'll be doing during the allocated time. Make this walk-through interactive so folks feel free to mention items you may have missed or to question activities they don't understand. This interactive agenda discussion will foster a shared ownership of the plan.

- Use it as a checklist for progress. We all like to see what we've accomplished, so use your agenda as a periodic progress check for the team. As you complete each agenda item, visually check it off. It's like looking at the map and marking that you just passed a specific point on your route. This will reinforce what's been accomplished so far and keep the momentum moving forward.

- Use it to postpone conversations that need to happen later in the meeting. It's typical for folks to want to talk about everything that's on their mind in the first ten minutes of the meeting. So when topics arise that are scheduled for later discussion, refer to the agenda and ask if the conversation can be postponed until then. To make sure these items don't get forgotten, notate the upcoming agenda topic with an asterisk (*) followed by the person's name. Also ask the person to take a moment and jot themselves a note so they'll remember their comments later.

- Use the agenda as a frame of reference for your action items. In the meeting documentation, group all the action items that resulted from the first agenda item together, then those from the second agenda item, and so on. This will help folks remember the context of the action items.

- Refer to the agenda from the previous meeting to bring continuity between meetings. Use it to remind your team what was accomplished in the last meeting compared with what was postponed and carried over to this meeting.

You'll find an agenda template to use as a starting point on the website.

Ground Rules

The problem with ground rules is they are often set but rarely used. These rules set the stage for how the team will interact during meetings. They enable any member of the team to remind the group of their agreements when they lose focus or need to be regrounded in acceptable behaviors. If the term *ground rules* doesn't work for your team, feel free to change it to something more appropriate, like *team operating principles* or *guiding practices*.

If this is an ongoing team, plan to spend part of your first meeting establishing the group operating norms: how we will make decisions, handle lateness, conduct ourselves during discussions, deal with nonperformance, handle interruptions (cell phones, laptops, pagers, text messages), and the like. Once created, have these available in every meeting and actively use them to manage group interaction.

But how do you actually use your ground rules to manage group interaction? By invoking them. Don't let the rules sit idly in front of the team. If you've agreed on a decision-making process, refer to the ground rules when you're ready to make a decision. If someone is late, pull out the ground rules and refresh everyone on the agreements. If someone consistently doesn't comply with the agreed-upon ground rules, talk to them on a meeting break and request that they honor the adopted operating principles. And be open to revising the rules as the team develops.

If this is a one-time meeting, we suggest you present the group with a set of recommended ground   rules rather than taking the time to create them from scratch. The website has a sample set of ground rules you can use as a starting point for discussion. Ask your team for their revisions and approval, making it clear that their agreement with these rules means that they will be used by you and other members of the team to govern the process as needed.

Action Items

Have you ever sat through a meeting in which commitments were made, only to find out no one wrote them down—and, worse, they were never acted on? Well, you're not alone. Only one in ten meetings tracked during the study of 150 corporate meetings included a follow-through process and clear communication of next steps (Ross, 2006). It's unfortunate, because these tasks are necessary to finalize the meeting goal or deliverable, but they require additional information or resources that aren't available in the moment. So postmeeting tracking and follow-through are critical. In our practice, we keep a running list of these tasks or action items throughout the meeting. Then before we leave the room each action item is reread, and someone from the team (one person, no more) is designated as the owner. That person provides a date by which the task will be completed, and you, in your role as project manager, track the item to completion.

Why just one owner and no more? So that accountability is clear. When there are multiple owners of an action item, it's easy to think the other person will initiate action—which ends up meaning no one does.

So how can this tool help the team maintain momentum and stay focused during the meeting? It helps you not waste time in discussions that can't be brought to completion in the meeting.

So if a conversation is going around in circles or taking longer than expected, here are a couple of questions you can ask to determine if you should cut the conversation short and assign an action item:

- Can we make this decision or come to closure on this discussion within the next ten minutes?
- If not, what information do we need or what action do we need to take to come to closure?

See the website for the template we use to electronically capture and track action items.

Parking Lot

The "parking lot" is a temporary storage place for ideas, concepts, desires, and thoughts that are tangential but often related to the objectives of the meeting. Although they may not be appropriate for today's meeting goal, they are definitely relevant to the overall project and will need to be discussed at some point. Just by making the team aware that such items will be "parked" or placed in a holding space for future conversation (in this meeting or a future one), you've established a mechanism for keeping the discussion on track. As these items come up, make them visible (on a flip chart, whiteboard, or projected screen) so the participants know their thoughts have been heard and captured. Attempting to ignore these related, yet slightly off-track ideas will ensure that they continue to come up randomly throughout the meeting, disrupting and delaying overall progress.

Tools for Clarifying Communication

Ever ask for directions, only to get an answer like "just drive down Peach Tree Lane until you reach the lot where the old schoolhouse used to be and head toward Um-Pah Lake on the fork"? The speaker thought the directions were clear, but who knows where the poor inquirer actually ended up? Understanding phrases and terms is critical to communication, and nearly every language is fraught with multiple meanings for each word. So we cannot assume that meeting participants truly understand each other when they attempt to communicate.

We recently observed a thirty-minute conversation in which four people were discussing an upcoming proposal to management. These were smart, educated people from diverse backgrounds putting forth their best effort in communicating with each other. Yet it took thirty minutes for them to realize that they were all in agreement about the proposal. The biggest surprise in this scenario is that it only took thirty minutes.

We all have terminology that we're comfortable with. I call it a cup; you call it a mug. I call it a plate; you call it a dish. Complicate that with phrases specific to our education and experience (for example, the term *development* has a different connotation to a human resource specialist than it does to a software analyst), then compound it with the company definitions and acronyms we learn as part of an organization. You can see why we're surprised that proposal discussion took only thirty minutes.

Now imagine that you have twelve people in a room trying to understand and be understood. You have another three participants who have joined by phone and a host of other people who will need to know what happened in the meeting. Suddenly, tools to help clarify communication in the room and clearly communicate the results afterward take on added importance.

Let's look at several of these tools to understand how we can better use them to ensure we're all on the same page.

A Glossary of Terms

As just illustrated, many of the lengthy conversations we've witnessed wind up being terminology related. To clarify communication, we must recognize when people use different words to describe the same thing. Perhaps even more challenging is the need to recognize that one word or phrase may have multiple meanings. The more quickly you can identify the puzzling concept or word, the more quickly understanding can be reached and progress made.

To help in this endeavor, some organizations have created a corporate glossary to define the myriad of acronyms and specialized terms they use. This corporate glossary is a handy starting place for a project meeting, but the need to define additional terms (or clarify existing ones) for better understanding is unavoidable.

Words and concepts are group dependent, meaning that each group of people will grapple with different things. As a result, each new project team will require its own glossary. At each meeting you can expect to encounter words and concepts that need clarification. And for the team to reach a shared understanding, these terms must be discussed, defined, and documented. So either create a meeting-specific or project-specific glossary of terms, acronyms, and phrases or agree on another source for your definitions. Agreement on these definitions ensures mutual understanding among those present in the meeting. Providing access to the glossary with the meeting documentation will provide additional clarity to those who were not in the meeting.

Here are some tips on the capture and use of the glossary that will further enhance understanding and communication:

- Capture the terms and definitions visibly during the meeting. Your goal is not to wind up with a precisely scripted, dictionary-worthy definition but to have a definition the team understands and can work with. They may need to play with the term several times before feeling comfortable that the definition fits. Have it visibly displayed for easy reference.

- Connect the glossary with the meeting documentation to clarify intentions and meanings for those not in the meeting. See the website for a template to use when electronically capturing a glossary.

- Accept the fact that the meaning of terms will gradually morph over the course of your project. Your glossary is a set of working definitions, so as you learn new things, the definitions may change. Update your glossary accordingly.

- As you document the meaning of a term or phrase, be sure to include any possible synonyms or aliases so that everyone can recognize more readily when they are using different terms for the same thing.

- Add to the glossary throughout the life of the project. Don't create a new glossary for each meeting. Instead, bring a copy of the terms defined to date to each team meeting and build on them as needed. This will aid in maintaining a consistent use of concepts and messages throughout project deliverables and documentation.

- Store the glossary with the project documentation. Some organizations have created online wiki's, websites, or blogs to promote viewing and maintenance of glossaries. Regardless of the access channel you use, the glossary should be viewable to anyone wanting to better understand the project.

Paraphrasing and Summarizing

At some point in your life you may have looked at a friend, colleague, or family member and asked them, "What did I just say?" Most often the response you get is a paraphrase of your original statement rather than the exact words. This interpretation (or often misinterpretation) of your remarks allows you to either repeat or rephrase your original statement so it's better understood.

Paraphrasing is a powerful tool. It provides a mechanism for the speaker and receiver to validate meaning and move forward with the assurance that they are in synch. Use this tool in your meetings to search for clarity when statements are vague or confusing. You can also use paraphrasing in the following ways:

- To regain control, try entering the conversation by paraphrasing the previous speaker. On confirmation of the paraphrase, move the group on to the next topic.
- Get a diffcult participant reengaged by asking the person to paraphrase what was just said: "Suzie, can you put that in your own words?"
- Check team comprehension by asking one of the team members to paraphrase what was said using terms more common to their line of work: "Dale, can you take a stab at rephrasing that, using words your financial colleagues would understand?"
- Validate that the speaker's point was really received by asking them for confirmation and giving them a second chance to restate their point: "Did Frank's paraphrase get at the heart of what you were trying to say? If not, can you try it for us again?"

Sometimes conversations bounce around so fast it's hard to keep up. When this happens, force the group to stop for a moment and realign by summarizing key points in the discussion thus far. Ask the team if your summary is correct and allow them to validate or correct it. Just like paraphrasing, this tool allows the team to continue discussion from a place of agreement around what's been said thus far.

You can also use the summarization technique to manage the pace of the meeting, validate the meeting notes, and clarify lengthy discourses. For example, you can:

- Bring a topic to a close by summarizing the highlights of what you've heard. Then move on to the next topic.
- Summarize by reviewing the meeting notes that have been taken during the discussion. This kills two birds with one stone, so to speak, by validating the notes at the same time as summarizing the conversation.
- Ask the speaker to summarize his or her own thoughts—especially when the comments were lengthy or involved multiple topics: "Barbara, can you sum that up in two or three sentences for us?" This will force the speaker to condense all that material into a meaningful nugget.

If It's a Virtual Meeting

Communication takes on a whole new meaning in a virtual world. "With virtual meetings, there is not even the need to pretend to pay attention," says Charles Parry, a principal at Signet in Boston. "Participants have a mute button and can read their e-mail to pass the time. So even if the meeting results in an agreement to take a certain course of action, some people who were 'in the room' may not have actually participated in, or even paid attention to, the decision" (Prencipe, 2001, p. 1). Virtual meetings force us, as PMFs, to get creative with how we manage meetings. We must not only employ all of the standard meeting practices but also add specialized techniques to foster nonvisual interaction and participation.

Our informal survey of project managers found that almost 60 percent of the meetings they attend are virtual, via conference call, videoconference, or web meeting (Resource Alliance, 2006). And all business trends seem to indicate that percentage will continue to rise.

So how do we make virtual meetings more effective? Since many minds are better than one, we asked our survey respondents about the techniques they've found most effective in

---

Maintaining Momentum in Virtual Meetings

"We have an average of 80 items to review every week in our sixty minute staff meeting. Our group is chatty and could spend the entire 60 minutes debating one issue. So I have instituted the Oscar music. Each week we have a special musical guest who sings if a team member spends more than 30 seconds on an item. It's a comical way to tell your team to keep it short."

Project Manager
Resource Alliance, 2006

---

making virtual meetings more productive. Here are some techniques both we and our colleagues have found helpful:

- Consider rotating meeting leaders or having phone attendees responsible for presenting or reporting.
- Over the course of the project, visit each team member's location and run the meeting from there.
- Have a visual of the participants so you can get a better sense of who you're speaking to. (We use a tool called a Meeting Roundtable; see the website for the template.)
- Have someone other than the person running the meeting be responsible for taking the meeting notes.
- Create a unique set of engagement rules specifically for virtual meetings. It can include guidelines such as team members identifying themselves when speaking ("This is Joe; I think . . ."), staying on mute when not speaking, not placing the phone on hold, and no more than one speaker talking at a time.
- Address people by name periodically throughout the meeting. Try to say everyone's name at least once during the meeting.
- Poll all participants for input. Seeking feedback from participants regularly during the session keeps them engaged.
- Summarize progress frequently throughout the meeting.

- Try using visual meeting software (such as WebEx or Web-Meeting) whenever possible to allow participants to see what is being captured or displayed electronically regardless of where they are physically located.

- Experiment with other collaborative web technologies to support specific meeting needs, for example, polling, voting, and synchronous discussion.

- If any of the meeting participants are located in the same city or building, consider having collocated participants meet together in a conference room and dial in to the meeting together rather than staying in their individual office spaces to attend the virtual meeting. These pockets of face-to-face groups can enhance the focus of all the virtual participants.

Notice that the critical issue for virtual meetings is participation. Although these meetings can save time and overall costs, they do so at the expense of the meeting leader. In virtual meetings, the meeting leader must work harder at keeping participants interested, engaged, and participating to make them effective—this, of course, means more time in planning and preparation.

Before you decide to go virtual, make sure it's a good fit for your audience, your objectives, and your abilities. To help determine which mode best fits your needs, see Table 3.1.

As the table indicates, you should use virtual meetings when they make the most sense, not just because you can. Psychologist Albert Mehrabian suggests that much of our communication is understood through unspoken indicators (Mehrabian, 1972). He suggests that

- 7 percent of meaning is in the words that are spoken.
- 38 percent of meaning is in tone and inflection (the way that words are said).
- 55 percent of meaning is in facial expression or posture.

TABLE 3.1

Should My Meeting Be Face-to-Face or Virtual?

Face-to-Face Meetings	Virtual Meetings
Face-to-face meetings are recommended when	Virtual meetings are a reasonable choice when
• There are complex objectives	• The objectives are simple or focused (one or two)
• Intense engagement with each other is necessary	• The meeting is to exchange information or make a specific decision
• The work requires an extended period of dedicated time to complete	• The work is more independent than interdependent
• Topics are highly political or sensitive	• The work can be accomplished in short spurts over a period of time
• There are extreme cultural differences	• The meetings are regularly recurring
• Diagrams, process maps, or other visual models will be built as a group	• The team members have known each other from previous projects or have met face-to-face
• The meeting is customized	• The group is geographically dispersed, and there is no opportunity for the group to join together face-to-face
• The group is collocated in the same area, city, or building location	

Source: Settle-Murphy, 2004.

That means that when we can't see each other we're getting only 45 percent of the picture (if that). Yet it is commonplace for two colleagues to sit within thirty feet of one another and communicate via electronic options rather than face-to-face. We email one another, IM one another, leave voicemails or text messages but rarely get out of our seats and walk to someone's office to have a conversation. With such a large amount of communication occurring through nonverbal modes, we need to be cautious when choosing the virtual path for our meetings. Keep this phenomenon in mind when planning meetings, and don't fall into the "virtual meeting" trap just because the technology is available to support it.

If There Are Telephone Participants in Your Meeting

Now what about those scenarios in which you've got ten people in the room and five others conferenced in? These situations are particularly difficult. Without careful management, phone participants wind up feeling like football fans without a ticket, standing at the gate unable to get in. Here are a few tips to enhance phone participation and inclusion:

- Ask all attendees (including those in the room) to state their names when they begin speaking.
- Create a name tent for the folks on the phone and set it in the middle of the table so everyone can remember they're present.
- Connect yourself or someone else in the room to IM so the remote folks can IM when they'd like to say something (if they can't break into the conversation any other way).
- Call on the phone participants at some point during each significant conversation. It may be that they want to join in but just can't be heard.
- Make sure conversation is verbalized—no head nods or other nonverbal body language.
- Do not mute the conference room phone to have exclusive conversations. This leaves phone participants feeling like less valuable members of the team. In fact, you may want to ask if you should leave the phone unmuted at breaks and lunch. Phone participants may want the freedom to join in on any conversations that might occur—business or otherwise.
- Remind people in the room that it is counterproductive (and just not fair) to continue the meeting after the phone folks have hung up.
- And, of course, use collaborative software so folks on the phone can see what's being captured in the room.

Tools for Sharing Meeting Results

There's a strange phenomenon in our world. People want—and in some cases need—to know what resulted from a meeting, yet people don't want to take the time to read the information. We can't totally overcome this problem, but we can communicate information in a manner that is more easily read and used. But how?

To answer this question, consider the world around us. Bookstores are organized by type of book—mysteries, fiction, travel, self-help. Grocery stores are laid out by type of food—frozen foods, produce, breakfast cereals, meats. Even this book is structured by category—just look at the table of contents. Science tells us that we do this naturally: to make sense of our environment, our brains attempt to meaningfully organize and categorize information. Categorization makes complex things easier to understand and navigate. It also provides easy access to the things we're most interested in.

So let's take advantage of that fact and report key information in categories rather than running streams of thought (like meeting minutes). Two tools that can help summarize and report information are the *one-pager* and *targeted meeting notes*.

The One-Pager

Like Sergeant Joe Friday on TV's *Dragnet* series, sometimes all our executives and stakeholders want is "just the facts, ma'am." So we're fans of the one-pager—summarizing key information on one page in either graphic, textual, or mixed formats. Dashboards, red/green project health reports, and even SWOT graphs (strengths, weaknesses, opportunities, and threats) are all examples of this tool. One-pagers allow your audience to pay attention to what's important or needs further action rather than wasting time on items of minor significance.

Another example that may be less familiar is what we call the *process change summary*. This type of one-pager is most useful for organizational change projects—describing the results of a process improvement or reorganization. It allows summarization of what's new or different, why it's beneficial, the challenges, and how those challenges will be addressed, all on one PowerPoint slide. See a sample of this template on the website.

Regardless of the format, one-pagers will bring the most benefit if you follow these guidelines:

- Make sure it's tailored to fit the specific needs and interests of those who will use it. If several audiences are the target of your communication, you may want to craft more than one one-pager to accommodate the specific information needs of each.

- Develop the one-pager together as a team to focus the group on the key issues. It creates a shared message that will then be spread by the team to the larger external audience.

- Use the one-pager when you have limited time to communicate progress and status. It'll force you to remain focused on the most crucial topics and help you remain true to your time limitations.

- Use the one-pager when the audience doesn't have a need to know further details. But always let them know how to access additional information should they want to know more.

Targeted Meeting Notes

Most meeting notes are random comments captured by well-meaning note takers who are making a judgment about what's important and what isn't. There's a better way. Let the team help determine what's important by giving them a way to make significant information visible during the meeting. There are six categories of information that seem to come up at every meeting: action items, assumptions, decisions, parking lot, learnings (these items will feed into your retrospectives), and glossary. So why not have a flip-chart page for each category already up on the wall in the meeting room (if you're face-to-face) or in an electronic document (if you're meeting virtually), ready to capture key items? In addition, you may have categories for content relevant to the project deliverable you're working on, such as assumptions, requirements, constraints, impacts, and dependencies. Prior to the meeting, think about the categories or types of information most likely to be discussed and have a method in mind for visibly capturing it, whether you're working virtually or face-to-face.

Next, align your meeting documentation with the information you captured in the categories. Have sections for assumptions, decisions, glossary, and so on. Good-bye, detailed meeting minutes; hello, useful information! Readers can easily scan the categories to locate items of interest rather than wade through volumes of superfluous data. Cut and paste appropriate sections into your tracking mechanisms for issues and action items and insert relevant content into formal project deliverables, but retain the original information as a meeting record.

Other Documentation Tips

Here are a few other keys to effectively sharing meeting information that we've learned over the years:

- View the meeting documentation through the eyes of an outsider. Assume you're reading the material for the first time. Is there content that needs a brief introduction to frame it appropriately? Do you need to describe anything about the meeting process to promote understanding?
- Consider the meeting substance as sacred. Although you may add an introduction or process explanation to provide clarity, do *not* change the meaning or intent of the material. The decisions, assumptions, and other meeting results were agreed to by the team and should reflect their thoughts.
- Make meeting documentation quickly available (we shoot for a twenty-four- to forty-eight-hour turnaround) and easily referenced to facilitate its use and keep the outcomes fresh in everyone's mind.
- Store project meeting notes with all the other project documentation.

Poor communication can ruin the best of intentions, as the following story illustrates. While in a store, a loving husband saw a set of four crystal wine glasses; the sign indicated a remarkably low price. Picking up four boxed sets, he smiled all the way to the register, knowing how surprised his wife would be at the purchase. When he finally got to the front of a long checkout line, the cashier asked, "You realize the price is *per glass* and not per set?" "Of course," he replied and strolled out. You can bet his wife was surprised, but over the price, not the intent.

Similarly, even the best participants in your meetings will at some point, although unsure about what's being said, nod their heads in agreement just so the meeting will move on. But at what cost? Without true agreement and understanding, the resulting actions can be costly. So apply these tools to make sure that communication truly happens or be willing to pay the price.

Summing It Up

Actively use these tools and techniques to help your group maintain focus and momentum throughout each meeting. But don't let them become the essence of the meeting. Consider the following when using tools and techniques:

- Don't confuse using a tool or technique with the goal itself. All of the tools mentioned here are intended to help you stay focused and manage the momentum of the meeting, but they do not ensure that you set the right goal.

- Remember there are tools to help you manage ideas, comments, and conversations that either are not in line with the meeting objectives or cannot be completed in the meeting. The parking lot and action item lists give you a place to hold these items and track them for future use.

- To ensure that two or more participants clearly understand one another, employ specialized tools such as a glossary, paraphrasing, summarizing, and the one-pager.

- For special circumstances, such as virtual and mixed-format meetings, use tools and techniques that keep unseen participants engaged in the meeting.

- Encourage face-to-face participation whenever possible. When using a non-face-to-face venue, take great care to make sure that what's *not being said* is still being *understood*.

- Summarize and categorize meeting results for better use and retention by those not in the room.

Chapter 4

Facilitation Tools for Keeping Everyone Engaged

> What brings me real joy is the experience of being fully
> engaged in whatever I'm doing.
> —PHIL JACKSON, National Basketball Association (NBA)
> coach and former player

HAVE YOU EVER EXPERIENCED a meeting that followed the agenda like clockwork—it started and ended on time, the attendees didn't chase tangents, it seemed that everyone was focused—yet results were lacking? Often lackluster results can be traced back to lack of engagement. Even a meeting that stays on track may produce poor-quality results if the attendees do not engage fully and stay energized to contribute their best work.

If a meeting is worth doing, it's worth doing well. And it's worth honing some techniques that will help you keep your meeting participants fully engaged in meeting activities. In our informal survey, 60 percent of the respondents cited "well-prepared participants" and "keeping participants engaged during the meeting process" as two of their top three contributors to achieving productive meetings (Resource Alliance, 2006).

How do you know if you're really getting the most out of the group? There's no single cue to look for, but there are a few telltale signs that team members have disengaged. Keep your eyes open for members who are

- Multitasking (using pagers, PDAs, or Blackberries)
- Coming and going from the meeting
- Contributing dialogue to topics that are already closed on the agenda
- Unable to respond when asked a direct question, without first asking you to repeat yourself
- Carrying on sidebar conversations with other participants
- Unable to restate key topics or decisions that were made in the meeting

These are just a few danger signals that indicate the group is not fully engaged in the content of the meeting. To get the most from your team, it's necessary to keep them actively involved in productive dialogue, idea generation, and decisioning.

Meeting Engagement Tools

An ounce of prevention is worth a pound of cure. Old saying—and still true. In the previous chapter we talked a bit about productive meeting preparation. That's where the seeds for effective participation are planted.

Preparing Participants to Be Productive

We know what you're thinking. You have enough to do to get *yourself* prepared to be an effective meeting facilitator—what can you possibly do to get the *meeting participants* ready to be productive? And is this really your responsibility? The answer is yes. If you subscribe to the concepts we presented in Chapter One, then you, the PMF, are responsible for the end-to-end meeting process: preparation, delivery, and follow-up. So yes, you'll need to not only prepare yourself but also determine how to best prepare your participants to be effective.

The preparation of participants depends on the type of meeting that you are convening. If the meeting is for information sharing only, then publishing the meeting materials in advance of the meeting may be enough to engage participants. However, if the meeting objectives include creative development or decision making, participants will need to engage with you in advance of the actual meeting in order to understand what is required of them. They may need to prepare their thoughts, obtain input from other colleagues, or bring necessary materials to the meeting. In complex meeting situations, you may need to meet personally with key participants to brief them on agenda details, discuss potential meeting derailers, determine alternate courses of action should difficulties arise, and solicit their commitment to full participation. Table 4.1 shows meeting types and some ways you can help your participants prepare to be productive.

Out-of-Meeting Coaching

Coaching employees to be their best is a significant portion of any leader's role. From the perspective of your role as a PMF, coaching also has its place. You encounter many levels of participation in meetings—good participants who give you what they have, mediocre participants who you know can offer more, and the occasional disruptive participant who almost derails your meeting. All of these may be candidates for out-of-meeting coaching.

This type of coaching involves a commitment of your time and typically needs to be done one-on-one. If your company policies or standards require an additional party be present during any coaching activity, then follow your best judgment and those standards. Arrange a time to speak with the person outside of the meeting environment and let the person know specifically what you are observing. Identify a goal to achieve specific to the person's participation and offer ideas on how the person could adjust that participation to

TABLE 4.1

Preparing Participants to Be Productive

Type or Purpose	Keys to Preparing Participants
All meeting types	• Be certain that the meeting invitation makes the meeting purpose and outcomes clear. • Clearly state in the invitation what is expected of the participants and how they will benefit from meeting outcomes. • Distribute the meeting agenda in advance. • Publish meeting materials in advance, if participants are to review and internalize the information.

In addition, consider the following specific recommendations:

Information exchange	• Get the meeting sponsor to send the invitation and agenda to the group. As this type of meeting is for sharing or dissemination of information rather than group decisioning, some participants may not recognize the importance of the meeting. Having the sponsor issue the invitation and agenda may carry the clout necessary to encourage full attendance and participation.
Creative development	• Contact participants prior to the meeting and discuss the outcomes that will be generated. Give them three to five questions to respond to prior to the meeting. Gather and compile these responses from key participants and use them as starting points for idea generation in the meeting as appropriate. • Contact key participants prior to the meeting to encourage preparation. Stress the importance of their contribution to meeting deliverables. Encourage them to think about the meeting topics in advance and bring any supporting materials with them to the meeting. • Discuss potential meeting derailers with key participants and determine how to avoid these and possible alternate courses of action.
Decision making	• Contact key participants prior to the meeting to encourage preparation. Stress the importance of their contribution to meeting decisions. Let them know what you need of them regarding decisioning. • Poll the participants prior to the meeting to determine what information must be available in order for them to make the meeting decisions. Use these findings to gather any additional information necessary for the meeting. • Ask these key decision makers to think about the meeting decision topics in advance and to bring any supporting materials with them to the meeting that will support their position. • Discuss potential meeting derailers with key participants, determine how to avoid these, and identify possible alternate courses of action. • Communicate the decision-making method. • Communicate whether the team will be making a decision or a recommendation.

TABLE 4.1

Type or Purpose	Keys to Preparing Participants
Coaching	• Provide any relevant background materials, goals, or objectives to the participants in advance that will help them understand expectations.
	• Ask the participants to provide their desired goals and outcomes to discuss at the session.
	• Call or visit the participants to invite them to the coaching session.
	• Provide a specific agenda and request that participants provide in advance any other topics that would be valuable to discuss.

interact most productively with the group. Provide input on how these changes will benefit the person as well as the larger group. Obtain a commitment from the participant to take action toward the improvement goal. Observe the participant's progress and schedule additional follow-up coaching as appropriate.

There are many coaching models available for the business setting. A well-accepted one is the GROW method (Whitmore, 2002), summarized in Table 4.2.

TABLE 4.2

Summary of the GROW Coaching Method

Coaching Step	Description
Agree on a Goal	Set a goal for future meeting participation. Make it clear and achievable.
Understand Current Reality	Be clear about the behavior that is being observed. Invite self-assessment by the participant.
Identify Options	Identify specific options for the participant to consider that will help him or her advance toward the goal.
Wrap up	Gain commitment from the participant that he or she will take action to change. Be specific about the behaviors that are to stop, or to start, in order to achieve the action plan. Clearly delineate next steps and a timeframe for achieving them.

Source: Adapted from Whitmore, 2002, pp. 53–56.

Soliciting Input Effectively

It's been said that opportunities are often missed because we are broadcasting when we should be listening: good advice to apply when facilitating. Gathering input from a group is useful to the extent that it is captured and presented in a way that the group can make use of it to accomplish their meeting objectives. This means active questioning and active listening on behalf of the facilitator. It also means intelligent capture and feedback of relevant dialogue elements to enable the group to *use* this information appropriately.

First let's look at the eliciting or "asking" side of the dialogue equation. When questioning is effective, people actively engage by composing responses—they recall ideas, link them to other ideas, reflect on them, and expand their understanding. As a project meeting facilitator, listen to understand, then question based on your understanding and group objectives. Questioning patterns are like a pyramid: start out simple to form the foundation, then build to the more complex questions within a topic. In fact, it may help to think of questions along a spectrum from low level to high level. Low-level questions tend to stimulate recall and bring out details and facts. High-level questions promote creativity and abstraction and encourage idea generation. They also stimulate synthesis and evaluation. Sequencing your questions intelligently, moving the group from simple to complex within a specific topic, will promote engagement and build comprehension.

In dialogue with the group you will use a variety of question types. Table 4.3 offers some suggestions for use of various questioning patterns when soliciting and clarifying input. Closed-ended questions are likely to solicit low-level results—details, facts. Open-ended questions lead more into high-level results. Listen for and challenge any limitations that the members place on themselves. Question the group to think beyond current constraints. And avoid compound questions—those that ask several things at once. People will respond to one question or

TABLE 4.3

Helpful Questions for Soliciting and Clarifying Input

Question Type	Consider Using This Question
Open-ended questions ► Have a variety of acceptable responses ► Encourage creativity ► Explore options	What have we observed in the last quarter that might prevent us from being successful in reaching the year-end deadline? How does that relate to what Joe just described? Can you elaborate on that comment? What are the possible reactions that might occur if we implement \<Decision A>?
Closed-ended questions ► Have a clear answer ► Quick check of knowledge ► Drive to a decision ► To confirm understanding	Are we in agreement on this? Who knows how often \<Situation X> occurred in the past month? Do we have data to support that observation? Who will take responsibility for this action item?
Leading/tag questions ► Bring people back to the task ► Check for understanding ► Lead the group in a certain direction	Can we move to this section of the agenda for a few minutes? We have fifteen minutes remaining. Can we take a checkpoint on progress? We didn't just say \<XYZ>, did we? So we're all in agreement on \<Decision A>, correct?
Challenging limitations ► Listen for words like "should," "should not," "can't," "ought" ► When ideas are not flowing	What would happen if you didn't do \<X>? If we don't do \<X>, what is the impact? (You may then want to explore how to address the key impacts.) If we adopt \<Decision A>, what are the benefits? What are the challenges? (You may then want to explore how to address the key challenges.) If there were no constraints on you, how would you \<X>? If you have all the resources you need, how might we do things differently?
Clarifying generalizations ► Listen for words like "never," "always," "all," "they," "only"	Never? Can you explain to us what causes you to believe this could "never" happen? Who are "they"? What information do we have that supports the assumption that \<X> would "always" happen?

the other, but rarely both, and never in the same order. So save yourself the headache and don't ask compound questions.

Let's look a little closer at the other side of the dialogue equation—listening. Dr. Joyce Brothers has said that listening may be the sincerest form of flattery. We believe that listening well is a true indicator of respect. And it is much more likely that your participants will remain engaged if they feel respected.

When facilitating, be other-directed—focus on the person who is communicating. Suspend your personal judgment regarding the content of their communication. Listen as a receiver and not as a critic. Support the speaker with minimally verbal responses—perhaps a head nod or a short verbal acknowledgment of a thought. Occasionally check for understanding. Paraphrase or summarize the speaker's words to integrate what is being said into the topic at hand. If, at any point, you sense that new information is contradicting previous information or decisions, bring that to the attention of the group and seek clarification and resolution. Listen attentively and intelligently.

Meeting Management Tools

So you've prepared well and addressed what you can to avoid problems. That's just a portion of what is needed to fully engage meeting participants. Within the meeting itself you'll need to manage the human dynamics carefully. As with our previous comments on facilitation, there is truly no cookbook here. Each meeting group is different. Add a participant or take away a participant and you'll experience a different set of human dynamics in the meeting. Even with the same participants, a change in topic or meeting type will change the dynamics of the group. Here are some tips for keeping the group actively engaged in the appropriate meeting activities.

Balancing Group Participation

So you're asking good questions and listening actively, but participation still does not seem balanced. One team member has not said anything the entire meeting, while two others continue to dominate the conversation. Kevin responds when you ask Jill a question. And Henry continually rephrases everything Carl says. Peter interrupts Nancy, and David has decided to check his text messages on his Blackberry.

There's no magic to keeping people involved and participation balanced. Everyone has an off day now and then. People can be distracted for many reasons, and most of them have nothing to do with your meeting. Still, you must make every effort as a facilitator to minimize disruptions and keep participants involved. If they believe their input is being dismissed or overlooked, they will withdraw from the meeting process, and valuable contributions may be lost.

Table 4.4 presents some tips for balancing participation in the meeting.

Enabling Decision Making

Leading people to decisions can be one of your most difficult challenges as a facilitator. You can lead, but you can't force a group to decide. Nor is it your role as a PMF to make the decision for the group. So prior to making a decision, confirm with the group what it is they're deciding on, then validate that the appropriate decision makers are in the meeting. If they are not in attendance, you have a couple of options. Capture an action item to follow up with the necessary decision makers or get the team to formulate a recommendation that then can be taken to the appropriate decision makers.

Let's assume you have the decision makers in the meeting. How can you lead them to make their decision? First, explore the problem or issue through facilitated dialogue. Allow open discussion and voicing of different opinions before asking participants to compare alternatives, summarize their ideas, and

TABLE 4.4

Tips for Balancing Participation

Situation	Consider Using This Question or Action
Multitasking, participants not paying attention	• Talk to participants in advance of the meeting and let them know that you need their full participation, especially at critical times. Agree on a phrase that you as a facilitator can say to call their attention back to the meeting ("Craig, here's where we really need your expertise . . ."). • If this is a virtual meeting, consider collocating participants who are in the same city with other participants in a conference room (supported by appropriate meeting technology). • If a participant is continually interrupted or called out of the room during meeting time, speak to the participant and request their permission to talk further with their boss (or whoever the interrupters may be). • Call the participant by name. • Call the participant by name and let them know that you're going to come back to them in a minute to get their ideas on the topic. • Use meeting technology to keep people on track, especially in a virtual meeting environment. • Ask the participants to turn off cell phones and pagers during the meeting session. • Ask the participants to put away their PDAs and use them only during breaks to prevent them from instant messaging each other across the meeting table or with folks not present in the meeting on nonmeeting-related topics. • As part of ground rules development, ask whether multitasking is OK. In some organizations, it may be not only OK but necessary.
You encounter the "dead zone"—excessive quiet from the group	• "We have some silence here—does that indicate <phrase>?" (such as "does that indicate that we're all in agreement?" or "does that indicate that we're not prepared to come to a decision on this?" • Call out the name of a specific participant who you know needs to weigh in on the subject, for example, "Sue, we haven't heard from you on this topic—what are your thoughts?" • Take the time to recap with the group—summarize progress and suggest where to go next or summarize progress and ask, "So, are we done with this topic? Can we move forward or do we need to action item something to do outside of this meeting?" • Take a break. Allow the participants time to regain their focus.

TABLE 4.4

Situation	Consider Using This Question or Action
Domineering or overactive participant	• Thank the person for their contribution and call on another person to contribute.
	• "We've heard from Ken and Nancy; can we get some input on this from other members of the team?"
	• "I realize this is a topic that you're passionate about, Carol. I'm sure a number of others are too; we need to give some time to those who haven't yet contributed their thoughts. Tom, any ideas?"
	• If the dominant participant is rehashing material or continuing to speak when his or her point has been made long ago, then interrupt, summarize the point, and state that we need to hear from other participants.
	• If two or three participants are dominating the conversation about something that is not entirely relevant to the meeting (such as too much detail), ask them to "take it off-line," then refocus the group with a direct question to another participant.
	• If too much detail is continually being offered, interrupt the person and say that the level of detail is not appropriate for this audience or purpose; ask the person to summarize so that we can move on with the meeting.
Sidebar conversations, multiple conversations	• Ask for "one conversation, please."
	• "We seem to have multiple conversations taking place—and from what I can tell they all seem relevant to the topic we are discussing. Take a minute and write down your thoughts so as not to lose them. Now, let's begin here in the front. Then we'll work our way around the table."
	• If face-to-face, walk over near the participants who are having the sidebar discussion—your physical presence may stop the sidebar.
	• Ask the participants to either focus with the group or to please take their conversation outside of the meeting room.
	• "I see that several of you have thoughts; let's start with you, then you . . ." Stack responders into a queue and take their comments one by one.
Interrupters and participants speaking for other participants	• Ask your question again directly to the person who was interrupted.
	• If one participant finishes another's sentences or interrupts and restates the answer, go back to the original speaker and ask if that view is consistent with theirs ("Karen, we just heard Bill's view—could you restate your viewpoint again for us, please?")
	• If the interruptions continue, take a break; speak privately to the interrupter and request that the behavior stop.

FIGURE 4.1

Dynamics of Group Decision Making

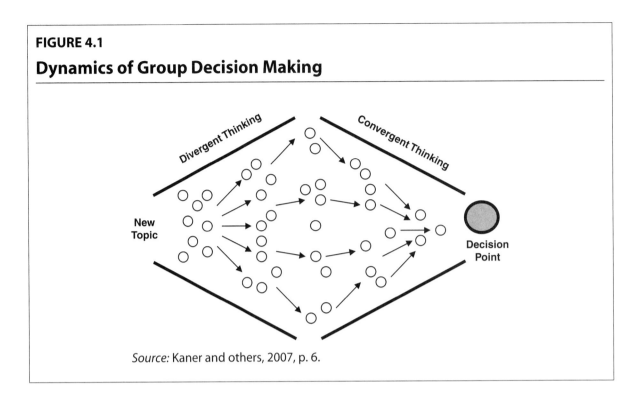

Source: Kaner and others, 2007, p. 6.

come to a conclusion. In his book *Facilitator's Guide to Participatory Decision-Making,* Sam Kaner refers to this as divergent thinking and convergent thinking (Kaner and others, 2007). Refer to Figure 4.1 for a visual of the divergent and convergent thinking pattern.

As a facilitator, you're doing a balancing act. You'll need to document points that are relevant to the decision during the divergent thinking stage, and you'll help the group evaluate ideas, summarize, and come to a conclusion during the convergent stage of decision making. There is no rule as to how much time this will or should take. While keeping the discussion focused, look for signs that all of the necessary information has been shared. Such signs may include a slowing of the dialogue or rehashing of points already made. You may also limit the discussion based on available time. Whichever way you lead the group from divergence to convergence, you'll need to understand the context of the decision and drive the group accordingly.

Help the group be objective in their decision-making process by using techniques that minimize emotional or political factors. These techniques will not make the decision for the group; rather, they can help the group organize relevant information and provide clarity to support their decision. Helpful techniques can include identification of prioritization or ranking criteria, force field analysis, use of impact matrices, pro-and-con lists, and gradients of agreement. See the website for the force field analysis, gradients of agreement, and impact matrix templates.

So is the group ready to make a decision? Table 4.5 provides some questions that you may find helpful as a facilitator when you need to get the group to decide.

What if the group can't make a decision, even after your best efforts to lead them there? Identify what the team needs (for instance, additional data, additional authority, time to think it over) to make the decision and come to an agreement on the next steps. Once the relevant information is in place to support the decision, you can reconvene the group, share the information, and again bring them to decision making.

TABLE 4.5

Questions to Promote Decision Making

- What else do we need to know or understand to make a decision?
- Do we have the right people in the room to make this decision?
- Is there something else that we need to clarify before we can decide?
- Do we have enough information to complete the decision on this item?
- I've heard several participants voice their agreement with <Decision A>; are there any objections to that decision?
- If we adopt <Decision A>, what will that do for us?
- If we postpone this decision, what will be the impact?
- I hear us leaning toward <Decision-A>; is that correct? Do we need any further discussion?
- What specifically is preventing us from making this decision?
- Can someone summarize our position on this issue?
- Are we ready to take a poll to see what we each think about <Decision A>?

Ensuring Ownership of Outcomes

As a facilitator, it is critical that you demonstrate neutrality and objectivity even when challenging or leading the group. It is essential that the team realize that ownership of the meeting outcomes lies squarely in their hands. To promote team ownership of results, here are a few techniques you can use:

- Keep all relevant meeting discussion points, analysis, and decisions visible to the group. If the team is face-to-face, this will likely be either on flip charts or projected electronically with a laptop and projector. If you have virtual participants, we suggest that you use appropriate meeting software so that participants can visually track with what is happening in the meeting.

- Reserve fifteen to thirty minutes at the end of the meeting to review accomplishments, action items, and decisions. Ask each participant to indicate verbally if he or she agrees with the outcomes and will support them outside the meeting room. (We have found that it's much harder for someone to distance themselves from the group agreements when they have verbally indicated their support.)

- Ask the participants to sign off on meeting outcomes to indicate their agreement (if standards or methodology require this level of formality).

- Do not change the content of meeting documentation outside the meeting session. Many facilitators feel the need to "clean up" the group outcomes, to reword or otherwise alter the meeting deliverables. Resist the urge to make changes to the documentation that was visible to the group during the meeting, or ownership will certainly be compromised.

- If a management debrief or checkpoint is approaching, engage one or more members of the team to present at the debrief on meeting outcomes. This solidifies ownership of outcomes by the team, rather than the project manager or facilitator.

Handling Difficult Situations

If you've been a meeting facilitator (or even a meeting participant) for very long, chances are you've encountered participants who are disruptive. Inappropriate meeting behaviors can quickly derail the entire group, unless the facilitator can intervene and get the meeting back on track. Any participant can display difficult behavior. Even the best participants have bad moments that can result in annoyance or frustration to the group. But that's not what we mean when we refer to difficult behavior. We mean habitual disruptive behavior patterns that are demonstrated repeatedly in group settings. Participants who demonstrate truly difficult behaviors do so because it works for them. It enables them to get what they want while controlling their environment and the people around them. "Although their numbers are small, their impact is large" according to Robert Bramson (1981, p. 3). He points out that "worst of all they appear immune to all the usual methods of communication and persuasion designed to convince them or help them to change their ways."

Difficult behavior can manifest not only as explosive or dominating actions within a meeting but also in silence or excessive agreement during a meeting, followed by rejection of meeting results outside of the meeting session. It is important for you as a facilitator to recognize occasional frustration in participants and separate those incidents from the habitual disruption imposed on a group by a truly difficult person. If you recognize habitual difficult behavior, keep three things in mind:

1. *Behavior that is rewarded gets repeated.* If you allow such habitual behavior to continue, it will continue. It does not self-correct.
2. *Stop wishing the difficult person were different.* You are not going to change the person. However, addressing the difficult behavior may change the way the person behaves around you.
3. *Change the team dynamics.* Sometimes behavior stops when the group begins to respond to it differently. It's as if a

dysfunctional family member has been allowed to continue destructive behavior; when the family dynamic changes, so does the behavior. So don't just focus on the squeaky wheel. Individually coach other team members about how to handle the behavior and respond to it productively.

Under no condition should you dismiss behavior that is having a negative effect on your meeting team. If the team senses that you are dismissing behaviors to avoid conflict, you'll lose the trust of the team and your credibility as a facilitator. You must be prepared to address the behavior. We are not encouraging you to embarrass anyone or take on the difficult behavior in a group setting but rather to be firm and clear regarding the meeting goals and apply techniques that will help the group stay focused and on track (see Chapter Three).

In difficult behavioral situations, it is always recommended to involve appropriate human resources support from your organization—they understand accepted personnel practices and can coach you in responses that are appropriate to your organization.

Summing It Up

- An ounce of prevention is worth a pound of cure. Pay attention to what participants need in advance of the meeting to do their best work in the meeting.
- Take the opportunity to engage in coaching. Helping others to recognize limiting behaviors and overcome them will benefit the individual and the team.
- Practice the powerful pairing of active listening and active questioning. Pattern your questions carefully. Challenge limitations and question generalities. The questions you ask and the way you integrate responses are critical to generating group understanding and enabling the participants to achieve their meeting objectives.

- Practice techniques that will enable you to balance group participation. Not everyone will speak the same number of words during a meeting, but everyone should be heard. Stay attentive to imbalance and address it.

- Be aware that groups will likely offer many opinions and options prior to evaluating, synthesizing, and coming to a conclusion. Don't short-circuit the process, but do stay aware of signs that it's time to converge and make a decision.

- Use appropriate techniques to organize information that is pertinent to decision making. Remember that these techniques won't make the decision for you, but they will help the group form a solid rationale for informed decision making.

- The meeting participants must own the meeting outcomes. Keep relevant meeting notes visible to the team, and don't reword outcomes after the meeting is over. Always obtain commitment to the meeting outcomes prior to adjourning the session.

Section II

Facilitating Meetings Within Each Phase of the Project

TIME TO GET TO WORK! There is no substitute for applying what you have read or learned to real-life situations. Look at every project meeting experience as an invaluable opportunity to refine your facilitation skills. There is no better way to improve your facilitation skills than to practice, practice, practice! Because your role as project manager assumes that you'll be holding and leading a variety of meetings, why not learn by doing—applying facilitation skills to your future project meetings?

Chapters One through Four provided the basics about meeting facilitation and tools. They highlighted the role of the project meeting facilitator (PMF) and outlined the facilitation tools and techniques that apply to all meetings—large or small, complex or simple. Now Chapters Five through Nine will take a look at the specific meetings that may occur within a project to better understand

- Where each meeting best fits in the project meeting road map
- Meeting purpose and objectives
- Suggested participants
- Typical inputs required for the meeting
- Expected outputs of each meeting
- Suggested agenda topics

To make this information easier to use in your everyday project life, we've combined these meeting detail tables found in each chapter into a master list—Project Meetings by Phase—which can be found on the website.

In each chapter, we'll provide an outline of where meetings typically fall in the framework of the project meeting road map. We've listed the phases: initiate, plan, execute, control, and close. The PMI publication *A Guide to the Project Management Body of Knowledge: PMBOK Guide* (*PMI*, 2004) suggests that these terms be used for project management *processes*, which occur within each phase of the project lifecycle (that is, within any phase you are actually initiating, planning, executing, controlling, and closing). Some authors in the project management field also have used these to name the overall *phases* of the project lifecycle. As you read through Section Two, we follow the pattern of introducing this terminology as the phases of the project.

Figure II.1 depicts the project meetings outlined in Chapter Two along with a recommendation of where these meetings fall within the framework of the five project phases.

We have shown the relationship between the sequential project phases and the meetings in Figure II.1. One point of clarification as we begin to discuss project phases and their corresponding meetings: we have found that many organizations work concurrently on certain aspects of project phases. This is

FIGURE II.1

Meetings Within the Project Phases

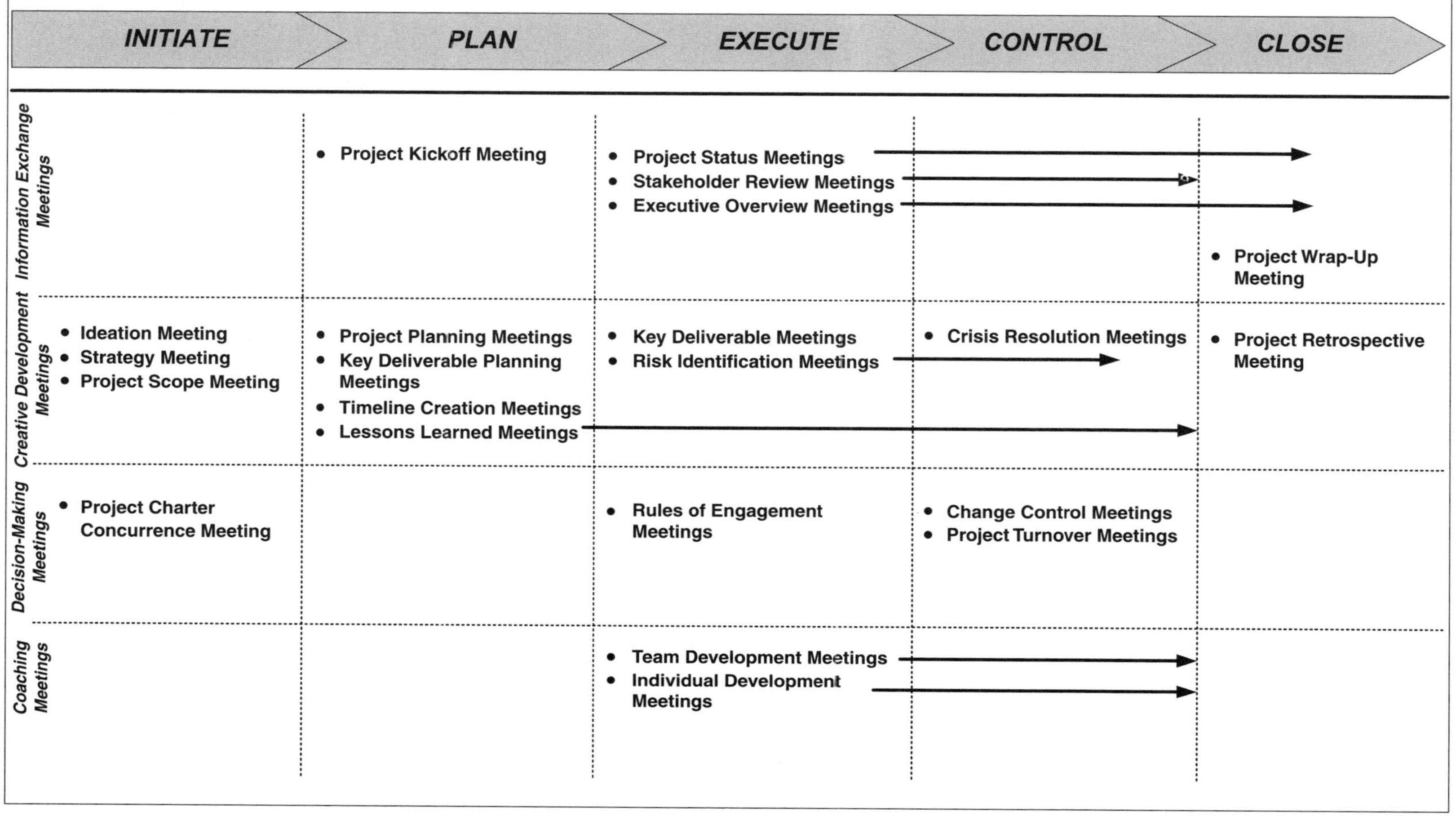

	INITIATE	PLAN	EXECUTE	CONTROL	CLOSE
Information Exchange Meetings		• Project Kickoff Meeting	• Project Status Meetings • Stakeholder Review Meetings • Executive Overview Meetings		• Project Wrap-Up Meeting • Project Retrospective Meeting
Creative Development Meetings	• Ideation Meeting • Strategy Meeting • Project Scope Meeting	• Project Planning Meetings • Key Deliverable Planning Meetings • Timeline Creation Meetings • Lessons Learned Meetings	• Key Deliverable Meetings • Risk Identification Meetings	• Crisis Resolution Meetings	
Decision-Making Meetings	• Project Charter Concurrence Meeting		• Rules of Engagement Meetings	• Change Control Meetings • Project Turnover Meetings	
Coaching Meetings			• Team Development Meetings • Individual Development Meetings		

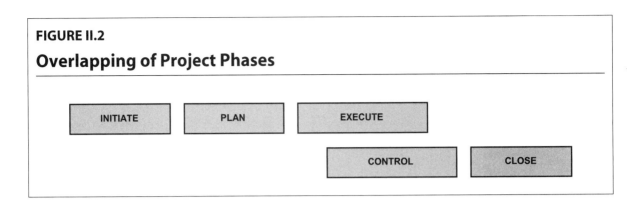

FIGURE II.2

Overlapping of Project Phases

often done to decrease the overall project duration, speeding up the time to market. Encouraging project teams to work on activities concurrently often results in the overlapping of the project phases depicted in Figure II.2. For example, many organizations begin to "control" the changes by holding change control meetings (see Chapter Eight) in the execute phase as soon as certain anchoring project deliverables have been officially approved. By overlapping these phases, project managers are able to influence changes earlier in the project, while the product is being built, rather than waiting to monitor change controls during post-build activities. As you can see in Figure II.2, the overlapping of phases differs from the more traditional waterfall approach outlined in Figure II.1. Keep in mind that with both approaches, the project meetings described in this book still need to take place—whether your organization follows the more traditional sequential phase or the overlapping phase approach.

We chose to use the Project Management Institute (PMI) project management process framework for our discussion because PMI is recognized as the leading organization for setting the standards for managing projects in organizations around the globe. We realize that there are a number of project lifecycle frameworks in the marketplace today. In fact, many organizations have developed their own internal project lifecycle phases to "chunk" the work into various groupings to assist with moving a project from start to finish. So you may have to translate the terminology presented here into that used by your organization.

There are a number of project meetings (both single point in time and recurring) that take place during the lifecycle of any project. Figure II.3 provides another view of the meetings that we will be discussing in the next five chapters. We refer to this model as the Project Meeting Road Map.

Ultimately, the application of project meeting facilitation is never complete unless you ask yourself what works well and what does not. Facilitators can have an excellent grasp of various techniques, but not knowing when to apply them to real-life situations can lead to disaster. At the end of each chapter in this section, you will find a list of what has worked well in these types of meetings and what hasn't. These nuggets come from our own client experiences and are presented to you with the intent of accelerating your learning and preventing blunders we've unintentionally made.

As you read each chapter, ask yourself. "What would work best in my situation?" Don't be afraid to step out of the norm and try something new or different. Great facilitators know when to make informed judgments and change direction in a meeting situation as appropriate; they do not simply follow a cookie-cutter approach.

FIGURE II.3

The Project Meeting Road Map

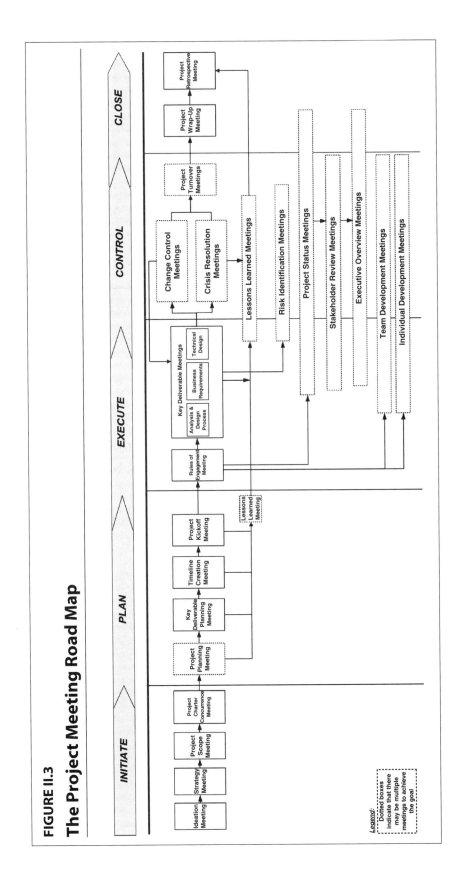

INITIATE   PLAN   EXECUTE   CONTROL   CLOSE

Ideation Meeting
Strategy Meeting
Project Scope Meeting
Project Charter Concurrence Meeting

Project Planning Meeting
Key Deliverable Planning Meeting
Timeline Creation Meeting
Project Kickoff Meeting
Lessons Learned Meeting

Rules of Engagement Meeting

Key Deliverable Meetings
Analysis & Design Process
Business Requirements
Technical Design

Change Control Meetings
Crisis Resolution Meetings
Project Turnover Meetings

Project Wrap-Up Meeting
Project Retrospective Meeting

Lessons Learned Meetings
Risk Identification Meetings
Project Status Meetings
Stakeholder Review Meetings
Executive Overview Meetings
Team Development Meetings
Individual Development Meetings

Legend:
Dotted boxes indicate that there may be multiple meetings to achieve the goal

Chapter 5

Facilitating Project Initiation Meetings

If your project doesn't work, look for the part that you
didn't think was important.

—ARTHUR BLOCH, author of *Murphy's Law*

INITIATE. THE MERRIAM-WEBSTER DICTIONARY defines initiate
as "to cause or facilitate the beginning of." As project meeting
facilitators and project managers, we are requested to do just
that whenever we engage in a project. However, organizations
often skip the initiate phase all together. This can lead to disas-
trous consequences.

Have you ever been in this situation? Someone stops you
in the hallway to run a great new concept by you. You listen intently and provide some constructive feedback about the
idea. A few weeks go by and you hear nothing. You may have
even forgotten about the hallway conversation. And then quite
unexpectedly, you are assigned as the project manager of "a
wonderfully new and exciting effort"—which, by the way, is
already behind schedule.

This happened to Joe, a new project manager at Allied
Corp. His new assignment was to launch the same new product concept that had been mentioned to him several weeks

earlier. He was told that his number-one priority, as the newly assigned project manager, was to coordinate a business requirements session. Being the good project manager that he is, he began to gather all of the existing documentation to understand the history of the project. He looked for documentation that would serve as an input into the requirements session—business case, purpose statement, project scope definition, project charter—only to find that none of these documents existed. His research uncovered that the project was launched based on a loose idea of a "business case," compiled from notes written down on the back of a napkin at an office social. The funding for the effort thus far has been with "some leftover monies from last quarter." He quickly found himself asking, "What happened? How did I get into this situation?"

Unrealistic? Hardly. As project managers, we have found ourselves in similar situations on more than one occasion. It is rarely fun or motivating to be part of something headed for disaster even before it gets started simply because of a faulty foundation.

Overview of the Initiation Phase

Initiating is defined by PMBOK (Project Management Body of Knowledge) as "those processes performed to authorize and define the scope of a new phase or project or that can result in the continuation of halted project work" (PMI, 2004). The meetings held and resulting activities performed during the initiate phase of a project are critical to the successful launch of the effort. It is important, before expending time and resources unnecessarily, that the business need is clearly defined and the basic framework regarding scope is documented and well understood. The outputs from the meetings held during this start-up phase serve as the anchor points for all future work done in later phases of the project lifecycle. One key deliverable or output of this phase, the project charter, serves as "the document that formally authorizes a project" (PMI, 2004).

So, by skipping the initiate phase and going directly to the gathering of requirements, our fictitious project manager Joe is setting himself *and* the project team up for a long and difficult road, if not certain failure. To avert disaster, Joe must stop, further assess the situation, and ensure that key initiate phase activities are completed. These activities will require a number of meetings. These meetings are held not just for the sake of holding meetings or to check off a task on the master task list but also to actually produce necessary deliverables. The project manager assigned to the new product launch needs to ensure that productive, well-facilitated meetings take place, resulting in tangible outputs that can be used going forward. These facilitated meeting outputs will help get the project back on track.

Project Initiation Meetings

You may be asking yourself, "Where do I begin?" There are a number of meetings that can take place during the initiate phase to help you get started. The four meetings we will focus on in this chapter are ideation, strategy, project scope, and project charter concurrence meetings. These are the ones most commonly requested by our clients. Figure 5.1 shows how these meetings fit into the project meeting road map.

To establish the foundation for future project work, these meetings (1) support the discovery of the critical business need or needs, (2) help define the purpose and objectives of the effort, (3) support the identification of what is in scope versus out of scope, and (4) help articulate how this project effort fits into the overarching strategy or vision of the organization. These meetings can also help redefine a project effort that was

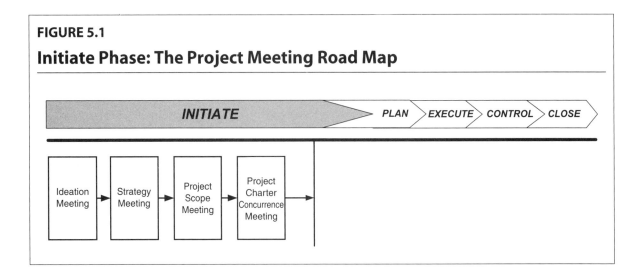

FIGURE 5.1

Initiate Phase: The Project Meeting Road Map

previously started but put on hold due to lack of resources, funding, time-to-market constraints, or a change in strategic direction. For example, holding a strategy meeting is one way to get a wayward project back on track and to refocus the effort of an existing project team while realigning the effort with the newly defined strategy.

The four meetings outlined in this chapter can be held individually or in some cases combined to get the same results. For example, combining the ideation and strategy meetings into some type of a hybrid version of the two meetings can result in ideas and suggestions about a specific topic while also allowing participants to evaluate the proposed business case. Table 5.1 provides a description of each meeting.

Each meeting has its own set of unique objectives. These meeting objectives need to be well thought out and included as part of the overall planning process for each meeting. In Chapter Three, we provided a Meeting Preparation Checklist (see the website for the complete Meeting Preparation Checklist).

At this phase of the project, many organizations have not officially assigned a project manager to coordinate the effort, as the project charter has not yet been approved. So just be aware

TABLE 5.1

Initiate Phase Project Meetings

Project Meeting	Type or Purpose	This Meeting Is Designed to	Objectives	Inputs	Outputs	Suggested Participants
Ideation meeting	Creative development	Gather participant ideas and suggestions about a specific topic without being constrained by artificial boundaries. The ideation meeting allows for a free, unconstrained exchange of ideas and thoughts regarding a specific business need or problem. This may result in suggestions for new or improved features, products, services, technologies, processes, or organizational structures.	• To understand the business problem or need along with its perceived drivers • To come up with possible strategies for addressing the perceived business problem or need	• Statement of business problem or need • Description of business strategy, vision (if available) • Available market, customer, and competitor analysis • List of individual ideas and thoughts (*if participants were asked to provide a sample list prior to the meeting*) • List of high-level predefined categories to spark conversation	• Validated or redefined problem or need description • List of categorized or prioritized brainstormed ideas • List of suggested improvements or strategies for addressing the need or problem • List of data needed to further assess the suggestions	• Facilitator • Potential project sponsor(s) • Potential project manager • Line of business stakeholder(s) • Marketing representative(s) • Subject matter expert(s)

(continued)

TABLE 5.1 *(continued)*

Project Meeting	Type or Purpose	This Meeting Is Designed to	Objectives	Inputs	Outputs	Suggested Participants
Strategy meeting	Creative development	Evaluate the proposed business case while reviewing analysis of data that either supports or does not support the suggested business need. The strategy meeting provides an opportunity for participants to determine if the suggested business need fits in the organization's strategic framework and vision.	• To determine if the business case warrants further exploration • To begin to frame the business case in light of the organization's strategic vision	• Output from any ideation meetings • Description of business strategy, vision (if available) • Data, reports, and other information needed to assess the business need or problem	• Business case draft • Statement outlining how the proposed project supports the overarching business strategy/vision • Formal recommendation to move forward or cease work on effort	• Facilitator • Senior executive(s) • Potential project sponsor(s) • Potential project manager • Line of business stakeholder(s)

Project Meeting	Type or Purpose	This Meeting Is Designed to	Objectives	Inputs	Outputs	Suggested Participants
Project scope meeting	Creative development	Allow participants to clearly outline the purpose and objectives of the proposed effort. The project scope meeting is ultimately held to clearly define the anchor points or scope that will frame the effort of work about to be undertaken.	• To clearly define the purpose for and objectives of the project • To draft the project scope and phasing of the effort	• Latest version of the business case • Business objectives and targets • Description of business problem or need • Notes from any preliminary scope discussions • Output from ideation and/or strategy meetings	• Preliminary scope, including proposed project purpose, project objectives, assumptions, constraints, and phasing	• Facilitator • Potential project sponsor(s) • Potential project manager • Potential product manager • Line of business stakeholder(s) • Marketing representative(s) • Technology representative(s) • Subject matter expert(s)

(continued)

TABLE 5.1 *(continued)*

Project Meeting	Type or Purpose	This Meeting Is Designed to	Objectives	Inputs	Outputs	Suggested Participants
Project charter concurrence meeting	Decision making	Provide a forum for participants to confirm and agree on the scope, proposed purpose statement, objectives, and key project drivers for the proposed effort. An approved project charter serves as the official sanction or start of a project and allows for continued planning, funding, and resource allocation.	• To confirm the business case • To finalize the project purpose and scope • To confirm the key drivers of the project from both a business and a consumer perspective	• Finalized business case • Data analysis to support the business case and customer needs completed to date • Preliminary project scope	• Confirmation of project scope • Agreed-on project charter document • Approval to formally fund the effort • Approval to engage a project manager	• Facilitator • Key executive(s) • Potential project sponsor(s) • Potential project manager • Potential product manager • Line of business stakeholder(s) • Marketing representative(s) • Technology representative(s) • Quality professional(s) • Subject matter expert(s)

that you may be tapped on the shoulder to take on the duties and role of a project meeting facilitator even when it's not your project (not officially, at least).

The Ideation Meeting

The intention of an ideation meeting is to allow free-flowing interaction around business issues. This discussion is high level and not intended to define requirements or solution details; rather, its overall goal is to establish the strategy on which a business case can be built.

Holding an ideation meeting should be considered optional. Ideation meetings are most effective when the business strategy seems murky at best, and further refinement or discussion of the original business idea needs to take place. However, if the business strategy is clear, this meeting may not be required.

Ideation Meeting Participants

Participants are those who contribute their knowledge and expertise to create the outputs and achieve the objectives of the meeting. This makes engaging the right participants a fundamental key to success (Means and Adams, 2005). And having the correct number of participants is just as important as having the right participants. Always keep in mind that the larger the group, the slower the progress of the meeting. This is especially true in a meeting in which the participants are passionate about the topic and need their individual thoughts to be heard.

Since this meeting focuses on the brainstorming of ideas and bringing some structure to those ideas, the fewer participants the better. If you can limit group size to five to seven participants, your time will be more productive. Table 5.1 provides a list of suggested participants that need to be involved in the initiation phase project meetings. Be aware that this is not an all-inclusive list and should be adjusted based on your organizational structure.

Ideation Meeting Inputs and Outputs

For the meeting to be most effective, there must be a clear understanding of the business problem or need before participants attempt to come up with possible strategies for addressing it. So make sure the team has an opportunity to get clarity around the issues before jumping into any brainstorming activity.

The meetings in this phase of the project typically follow a sequential order. In other words, the outputs from the ideation meeting will be carried forward as an input into the project strategy meeting.

Ideation Meeting Standard Agenda

This meeting can take up to four hours, but can be broken into two discrete two-hour segments if necessary. The topics to address as part of this meeting include

- Clarification of the business need and associated drivers
- Identification of decision-making criteria—a discussion around how we'll be able to evaluate which strategies best fit our needs, goals, and desires
- Identification of possible strategies to address the need or provide the desired benefits
- Prioritization of strategies based on decision-making criteria
- Discussion of actions to further investigate or validate the business case based on the highest-priority strategies

Ideation Meeting: Face-to-Face or Virtual?

Because the ideation meeting falls under the heading of creative development–type meetings, it is strongly recommended that they be conducted face-to-face, with no phone participants. However, these meetings can be held virtually if you use collaborative software (such as WebIQ, GroupSystems, or FacilitatePro) that allows group brainstorming, categorizing, and ranking.

The Strategy Meeting

Between meetings, work has progressed on the business case. Data has been analyzed and financials reviewed to assess the strategies defined in the ideation meeting. Now you're ready for the team to reassemble and look at the results to determine whether the suggested case fits in the organization's strategic framework and vision.

This meeting is helpful for most projects, as it allows discussion of the elements surrounding the business case. If an ideation meeting wasn't held, you may need to use this opportunity to identify additional analysis or investigation required to create a draft.

Strategy Meeting Participants

As for the ideation meeting, the number of participants for the strategy meeting should be small (approximately five to seven participants). Some of these attendees—key executives, the project sponsor, and senior line of business leaders—will not be involved in the day-to-day activities of the project; however, capturing their input about the direction, vision, and scope of the effort is critical.

Strategy Meeting Inputs and Outputs

Your goal is to leave this meeting with a first draft of the business case. To do that, you'll need the output from the ideation meetings and other discussions held or work done around the business issue, drivers, and supporting data analysis. All this information will be discussed and transformed into a business case that defines how the proposed project supports the overarching strategy and vision of the organization.

Strategy Meeting Standard Agenda

Depending on the scope of the proposed project and the depth of work that has been completed so far, this meeting could range anywhere from four hours to two days. However, since creative development of the business case requires focused attention, you may want to approach it in segments of four hours to allow a break between meetings for recharging the brain and performing additional research. The topics to be covered during the meeting include

- Review and validation of the business need and associated drivers
- Discussion of the long-term vision of the organization as it pertains to this area of the business
- Development of a proposed strategy to address the need; this should include a statement of how the strategy will support the overarching business vision and goals
- Delineation of the anticipated costs, benefits, impacts, and timing

Strategy Meeting: Face-to-Face or Virtual?

The strategy meeting is best held face-to-face. When working on strategy or vision statements in this setting, it is helpful (especially for your participants who are more visual learners) to be able to not only hear the ideas expressed by their colleagues but also see them displayed. So we recommend the use of a projector to display the computer screen contents electronically in conjunction with sticky notes on flip charts. These two techniques combine very effectively to display the large amounts of data that these types of meetings can generate. Either method provides the flexibility needed to move or to rearrange ideas into categories or to reorganize the information as the meeting progresses.

As with the ideation meeting, you can conduct strategy meetings virtually using collaborative software. But to keep them effective, you will need to condense the meeting length (requiring more meetings), and you'll need to focus each meeting around just one or two topics from the agenda.

The Project Scope Meeting

The project scope meeting begins the process of officially defining the anchor points or scope that will frame the effort of work that is about to be undertaken. The more detailed the results are, the easier it will be to develop and ultimately confirm the project charter. This meeting is a necessary part of every project and should not be overlooked.

Project Scope Meeting Participants

Ideally, we suggest limiting meeting participation to eight to twelve people, especially when the meetings are for creative development or decision making. However, this does not mean that those eight to twelve people are the only ones to provide input into the final deliverables. You may need to schedule a follow-up meeting to review the output of the core group with a larger team. If you hold a follow-up meeting and you have promised to incorporate input from additional participants, you need to do it. One of the fastest ways you can lose credibility as a PMF is to promise to do something and then not deliver. If you don't follow through, you not only risk losing credibility, but you may also incur a graver consequence, which will impact future meetings: people declining to be involved or participate in meetings that you facilitate.

It is also a good idea to include someone from your technology area in the project scope meeting, especially if the project involves a change requiring technical development or support. You may ask, "Why would I include someone from technology at this early stage in the project? Wouldn't that be a waste of their time before we really know our scope or requirements?" Both our experience and studies performed on software development projects have demonstrated that the earlier your technology partners are involved in the process, the better. In his 2000 study *Software Assessments, Benchmarks, and Best Practices*, Capers Jones found that holding cross-functional meetings (that included technology representatives) early in the project not only reduced the risk of scope creep from 80 percent to 10 percent but also reduced the overall project elapsed time and workforce effort by 5 to 15 percent (Jones, 2000).

Your technology partners can serve in an advisory capacity to inform the team of impacts on cost and development time and options. This information can be useful to the other participants responsible for making recommendations and decisions concerning the scope of the effort. And don't underestimate the value to the overall project cycle time. Hearing firsthand what the business is thinking helps your technology partners better understand your intent, start to think about implications to other projects, and plan for delivery. For a complete listing of project meeting participants and a definition of their role, please see the suggested meeting participants and role definition matrix on the website.

Project Scope Meeting Inputs and Outputs

This is your first attempt at putting some boundaries around the size and breadth of the effort you're undertaking, so come armed with the latest version of the business case and some idea of the categories you may need to scope. For instance, you may need to discuss the geographic region this project will apply to. Will it be international or just domestic? If international, will it include all countries or will some be excluded? The categories you need to consider will vary depending on the type of project, but some examples are type of customer (retail, wholesale, private, military, small business, and so on) and method or channel of entry into the process (Internet, walk-in, phone, mail, fax, and so on).

Based on this discussion, you will develop a preliminary scope. This is more than just a scope statement; it should include as many details around what's included and not included as is possible at this point. It should also include a proposed purpose statement for the project, its objectives, and any assumptions or constraints that are known. If the project is going to occur in stages (for example, we'll roll it out in Australia and the United States, followed by Europe), you'll also want to include that as part of the scope.

Project Scope Standard Agenda

This meeting works best if everyone can devote up to four hours to the effort. The topics to address as part of this meeting include the following:

- Definition of the project purpose and objectives
- Discussion of what's in and out of scope for the project, along with the rationale for those things believed to be out of scope
- Delineation of any known assumptions or constraints
- Discussion of project staging, if needed
- Identification of any items needing further investigation to determine whether they're in or out of scope

Project Scope Meeting: Face-to-Face or Virtual?

This meeting is more workable in a virtual setting than either the ideation or strategy meetings. Its content is more tangible, and with the use of NetMeeting or similar web-based tools, virtual participants can see what's being captured. But we still strongly recommend that the project scope meeting be held face-to-face, if at all possible, especially if the project is large and complex.

The Project Charter Concurrence Meeting

The business case has been finalized, and based on it, a project charter has been drafted. This charter will serve as the anchor point for the project. All future work will be built on its foundation. So getting agreement on the charter content is critical! Hence the need for a project charter concurrence meeting. This meeting brings the key stakeholders together to finalize the project charter and get their approval to move forward to the next phase of the project.

Participant Contact List

Once you've identified the meeting attendees, create a Participant Contact List. You can use this list for several valuable purposes:

- To ensure all business areas are represented
- To record acceptance of meeting invitations
- To identify which participants will be face-to-face and which will be participating by phone
- To take attendance in the meeting and ensure that your key participants are present

---

Project Charter Concurrence Meeting Participants

Because the project concurrence meeting is a decision-making meeting requiring a wider audience for input and approval, the number of participants may be closer to twelve to fifteen. Again, the more people at the meeting, the more time it is likely to take to accomplish the meeting objectives. So choose participants wisely. It is important that the right decision makers (such as key executives, potential project sponsors, and line of business personnel) are invited to take part in the meeting. And for the same reasons mentioned in the project scope meeting discussion, it is a good idea to include someone from your technology area, especially if the project involves a change requiring technical development or support.

Review the list for completeness and ask yourself key questions such as the following (see the website for the Key Participant Checklist):

- What role does this person play in the project?
- What insight does this person bring to the discussion?
- What role will this person play in the meeting?
- Does this person have the authority to make decisions?
- Can the meeting take place if this person is unable to attend?

After you have satisfactorily answered these questions, send out the official meeting invitation to those on your Participant Contact List (see the website for an example Participant Contact List).

Project Charter Concurrence Meeting Inputs and Outputs

The outputs from the previously held meetings serve as inputs into the final project charter concurrence meeting. It is important to continue to update the documentation as changes are made, so that the latest versions are carried forward into this meeting. The result of this meeting will be a confirmed project charter, along with the approval to formally fund the effort and hire a project manager (if one has not already been assigned).

Project Charter Concurrence Standard Agenda

To minimize the amount of time required for this meeting, a draft of the project charter should be sent to all participants ahead of time. It is expected that they'll come prepared to discuss only those areas with which they are not comfortable. With this expectation, the meeting will likely last no more than two hours.

The topics to address as part of this meeting include the following:

- *Roll call.* The names of all participants and the areas they represent.
- *Identification of what's to be discussed.* Ask the team which sections they think need further discussion or clarification. This question is based on the assumption that they've done their prework.
- *Discussion of issues.* Walk through each section of the charter that was identified and revise it as needed to reflect the shared agreement of the group.
- *Verbal confirmation of agreement with charter.* This may be followed up with formal signatures if needed.

- *Identification of issues needing further follow-up, if needed.* If anyone is unable to agree with the charter, ask the person, "What do you need to see or understand in order to provide your confirmation?" Document this as a follow-up task and get the person's provisional agreement based on seeing the results.

Project Charter Concurrence Meeting: Face-to-Face or Virtual?

As discussed in Chapter Four, managing group dynamics and soliciting input effectively from your participants is critical to the success of decision-making meetings. Because strong facilitation and consensus-building skills can make or break a decision-making meeting, it is also recommended that the project charter concurrence meeting be held face-to-face. By holding a face-to-face project charter concurrence meeting, the PMF can read those nonverbal cues and better gauge participant involvement and agreement.

Troubleshooting Guide

What Works and What Doesn't Work

Experience is a wonderful teacher, but we hope to help you bypass some of the more unpleasant learnings by sharing what we have found that works well in certain meeting settings and what does not (see Table 5.2).

TABLE 5.2

Initiate Phase Meetings: What Works and What Doesn't

Project Meeting	Type or Purpose	What Works	What Doesn't Work
Ideation meeting	Creative development	• Providing an opportunity for all voices to be heard—a great way to get an open, honest exchange of ideas • Creating a safe environment for participants to share information • Allowing participants to make suggestions without fear of repercussion or constraints	• Continuing to force the generation of ideas once the "well is dry" • Cutting off or negating a participant's ideas while still in the process of gathering ideas • Forcing a group to categorize their ideas too early in the process
Strategy meeting	Creative development	• Allowing participants to focus on the overall vision and strategy of the organization • Including the right level of participants for a strategy discussion	• Allowing participants to manipulate data to support the business case just to get an effort funded
Project scope meeting	Creative development	• Allowing participants to openly discuss the pros and cons of scope-related items • Capturing measurable project objectives that support business objectives and targets • Capturing the scope rationale for items that are excluded from the scope (so that the reason for excluding a scope item is documented for future reference)	• Forcing a group to nail down the scope to adhere to a predefined agenda timeline • Not allowing a group to update the scope definition once answers to outstanding questions and action items are known
Project charter concurrence meeting	Decision making	• Confirming that the proper level of decision makers will be at the meeting and are prepared to make those important decisions • Realizing and communicating that the scope is still a work in progress; the entire scope statement or table will need to be reviewed and confirmed as part of this meeting	• Assuming all participants have the same understanding of the business need • Assuming that participants have read all documentation sent prior to the meeting • Allowing discussions to take place around possible solutions

(continued)

TABLE 5.2 *(continued)*

Project Meeting	Type or Purpose	What Works	What Doesn't Work
		• Making the team aware that the output from this meeting will be used to formally launch the project effort	• Beginning to capture detailed requirements rather than confirming the project scope • Allowing participants to postpone scope decisions until a future date

We look forward to you adding your own experiences to this list as you grow in your meeting facilitation skills. During the initiate phase of the project, here are several key things to do or avoid:

- *Do* ensure you have participants with the right authority and knowledge level at each meeting.

- *Do* create a free and open environment for your participants to express their ideas.

- *Don't* allow participants to manipulate data to support a weak business case.

- *Don't* dive into requirements building. This comes well after setting the scope and finalizing the project charter; it will be addressed in a later project phase.

- *Don't* allow discussions to center around possible solutions too early in the process.

Troubleshooting

In Table 5.3 you'll find a list of some common problems that arise when facilitating meetings in the initiate phase of a project. We have outlined each problem and offer some possible solutions to assist in overcoming them.

TABLE 5.3

Troubleshooting Guide for Initiate Phase Meetings

Problem	Possible Solutions
The project was previously started but put on hold. How do we get it started and refocused?	• Hold a strategy meeting to reevaluate the business case in light of the current environment.
What if the suggested participants are not available for the project charter concurrence meeting?	• Reschedule. You do not want to move forward without full concurrence on the project charter.
What if the suggested participants are not available for the ideation, strategy, or scope meetings? Does the same rule apply as with the project charter concurrence meeting?	• Not necessarily; for these meetings you can consider iterative development of the outputs. Hold a meeting with the participants that are available to draft the outputs. Review it with the missing participants to get their input either off-line or in a separate meeting. Hold a final meeting for validation either in person or virtually, using meeting support technology so everyone can give their input.
What do I do if I'm assigned a project, but there is no project charter and I'm being pressured to hold a kickoff meeting?	• Stop and take a step back. At a minimum, you must hold a project scope meeting and a project charter concurrence meeting. Otherwise, without a finalized project charter, you really do not have any authority to hold a kickoff meeting because the project, in theory, has not been officially sanctioned.
What should I do if risks, requirements, or possible solutions come up during our meeting discussion?	• Capture the risks, requirements, or possible solutions on a flip chart so folks know that you've heard them, then guide the group back to the topic at hand. • Transfer this information into an electronic spreadsheet and continue adding to it throughout the project lifecycle. • When you get to the appropriate phase of the project, introduce these items as starting points for discussions in meetings such as risk identification, requirements definition, and the like.

Chapter 6

Facilitating Project Planning Meetings

If you don't know where you want to go, you might end
up some place you don't want to be.

—ANONYMOUS

AT THIS POINT YOU SHOULD have an officially sanctioned
project with an agreed-upon project charter—complete with
confirmed purpose, objectives, and baseline scope of the effort.
So you're ready to hold that much requested and anticipated
requirements meeting, right? Wrong.

Sometimes the pressure to jump from confirmation of the
project charter into full-blown requirements can be overwhelm-
ing. This pressure can stem from both the project sponsor and
the line of business representatives who feel their pressing business needs must be resolved quickly. But beware—excessive
schedule pressure is a key contributor to poor quality, canceled
projects, low morale, fatigue, burnout, and high attrition rates
(Jones, 1994). So when asked why you're taking valuable time
to *plan* the work rather than just *doing* it, remind them that lack
of planning is one of the top two reasons for project failure (IT
Cortex, 1998).

Continuing our story of Joe, the project manager for the new product development effort, you can certainly understand his dilemma. He was already under time pressure because his effort was behind schedule when he inherited it. In spite of this, he had stalled for time to go back and build a foundation for the project by completing the initiate phase deliverables. So why not just jump into the requirements-gathering process and get on with it?

Overview of the Plan Phase

The plan phase is intended to "define and mature the project scope, develop the project management plan, and identify and schedule the project activities that occur within the project" (PMI, 2004). When working with clients, we often refer to the steps involved in planning as developing the road map for success. Without an adequate road map, success can be elusive.

Imagine for a minute that you are going to drive across country, from Washington, D.C., to San Francisco, to visit your sister. You are confident of the purpose of your trip and even know what your final destination is. Would you want to leave your home without a map? Without hotel reservations? That depends on your goal. You would probably experience a few course diversions and bumps in the road, but you would eventually get to San Francisco. Great! A carefree experience like this might be fun. But what if your goal was to get there for her surprise fortieth birthday party? The introduction of an immovable arrival date transforms the carefree journey into one you might find stressful and expensive, something you'd rather not repeat, unless you take the time to plan the trip.

The only way to ensure your timely arrival at the destination is to plot out your route, check on weather and road conditions, make hotel reservations, contemplate contingencies, and based on all that, build an itinerary or plan. By taking the time to create this road map for your trip, you can estimate the duration of the trip, the number of planned stops, and how much money you will need for fuel, food, lodging, and even emergencies (such as a flat tire), and you would possibly limit some of the unexpected hurdles you could encounter.

Projects are a lot like road trips. There are certain things you know once you have a finalized project charter (purpose, objectives, scope), and there are certain things that you can estimate (potential resources, timeline, and budget), but there are still many unknowns or unexpected roadblocks (loss of resources to other projects, change in strategic direction, scaling back of scope, budget cuts). However, by placing the proper attention on planning, you can create a road map for success that will better equip you for handling those unexpected diversions, delays, and bumps along the way.

At this point, you may be saying to yourself, "Geez, this sounds like a lot of work!" In fact, it is. The work that takes place in the plan phase is often the most underestimated and overlooked of all of the phases. The overarching goal of the plan phase is to create your road map for success. With the proper planning, the subsequent project phases will be much smoother, and you will have more confidence in your ability to overcome any unexpected hurdles thrown in your way.

Project Planning Meetings

The five meetings we'll discuss in this chapter expand the foundation that was begun in the initiate phase of the project. These meetings begin to truly outline what steps need to be taken to turn the business objectives and scope statement into reality. This involves taking the time to align the necessary resources for the scope of the effort, ensure that the key subject matter experts are included in the project kickoff meeting, and validate the proposed timeline. These meetings also provide a forum for gathering insights about the project as it progresses and ensuring that the necessary project deliverables have been identified. The meetings included in the plan phase are

- Project planning meetings
- The key deliverable planning meeting
- The timeline creation meeting
- The project kickoff meeting
- The lessons learned meeting

Figure 6.1 shows the various meetings and their interrelationships.

These meetings encourage creative development of a deliverable or solution through thoughtful discussion, debate, or input. Table 6.1 provides a description of each meeting we'll be talking about in this chapter.

FIGURE 6.1

Plan Phase: The Project Meeting Road Map

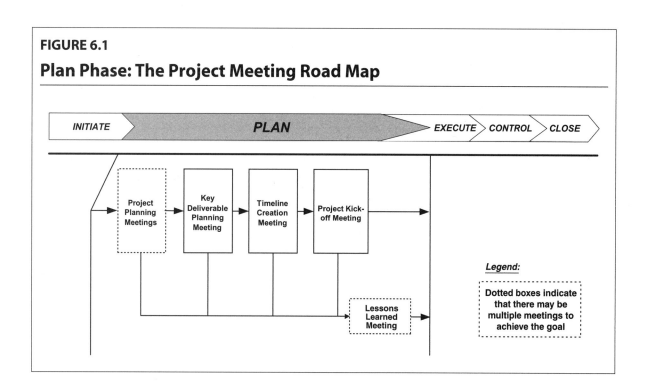

TABLE 6.1

Plan Phase Project Meetings

Project Meeting	Type or Purpose	This Meeting Is Designed to	Objectives	Inputs	Outputs	Suggested Participants
Project planning meetings	Creative develop-ment	Allow the project manager to meet with those identified as part of the core project team (may need to meet multiple times) to begin to identify potential subteams and to align resources with the overall purpose and scope of the effort based upon the finalized project charter.	• To confirm core project team members • To identify extended project team members • To develop presentation materials and agenda for the kickoff meeting	• Finalized project charter • List of potential core and extended project team members • Notes from all preliminary project planning meetings	• Agreed-upon list of core team and extended project team members • Finalized kickoff meeting agenda • Finalized kickoff meeting presentation materials • Baseline recommendations for potential subteams and possible subteam members • High-level project road map	• Facilitator • Project sponsor(s) • Project manager • Product manager • Line of business stakeholder(s) • Technology representative(s)
Key de-liverable planning meeting	Creative develop-ment and decision making	Determine and confirm the key deliverables that are required to support the effort and agree on a standard format in which the deliverables will be created.	• To identify nonnegotiable key deliverables and the meetings required to create the key deliverables	• Updated list of assumptions, constraints, dependencies • List of any outstanding timeline concerns	• List of nonnegotiable key deliverables • List of key deliverable meetings and target completion dates (analysis and design meetings,	• Facilitator • Project sponsor(s) • Project manager • Product manager • Project management office representative(s)

Project Meeting	Type or Purpose	This Meeting Is Designed to	Objectives	Inputs	Outputs	Suggested Participants
			• To align individual key deliverable meetings within the agreed-upon project timeline • To identify baseline objectives for each of the individual key deliverable meetings • To confirm a project team owner for each of the key deliverables • To agree on standard format of key deliverables	• Proposed list of roles and responsibilities • Finalized list of subteams and subteam members • List of standard project deliverables, if one exists, or list from similar type of project • Sample deliverable templates, if they exist	business requirements meetings, technical design, implementation approach, communication approach, training approach, and so on) • Updated proposed list of roles and responsibilities, with potential key deliverable owners identified • Agreed-upon key deliverable formats	• Subteam owner(s) • Line of business stakeholder(s) • Marketing representative(s) • Technology representative(s) • Quality professional(s) • Legal representative(s) • Compliance representative(s) • Subject matter expert(s)

(continued)

TABLE 6.1 *(continued)*

Project Meeting	Type or Purpose	This Meeting Is Designed to	Objectives	Inputs	Outputs	Suggested Participants
Timeline creation meeting	Creative development	Allow the project team to think through the key project milestones in an interactive way. This meeting provides a forum for all participants to discuss concerns, assumptions, constraints, and dependencies and to look at potential mitigation strategies to overcome timeline-related issues (sometimes this meeting is held in conjunction with the project kickoff meeting).	• To visually depict the size of the effort and time needed to complete the effort • To uncover unrealistic dates and overlapping activities • To identify key constraints and dependencies • To discover conflicts between the timing of project, operational, technology, and potentially vendor timelines and activities that are occurring concurrently	• List of all known assumptions, constraints, dependencies • List of any scheduled enterprise application release dates • High-level project road map • List of key deliverables • Known resources	• Agreed-upon project milestone timeline • Updated list of assumptions, constraints, dependencies • Timeline rationale • List of any outstanding timeline concerns	• Facilitator • Project sponsor(s) • Project manager • Product manager • Subteam owner(s) • Line of business stakeholder(s) • Marketing representative(s) • Technology representative(s) • Quality professional(s) • Legal representative(s) • Compliance representative(s) • Subject matter expert(s)

Project Meeting	Type or Purpose	This Meeting Is Designed to	Objectives	Inputs	Outputs	Suggested Participants
Kickoff meeting	Information exchange	Provide an opportunity to introduce the effort to the core and extended project team members. This meeting generally serves as the official beginning of project meetings that involve the core and extended project team members who will be responsible for implementing the project.	• To review the finalized business case • To review the finalized project purpose and scope • To review the key drivers of the project from a business and a consumer perspective • To discuss a potential project timeline • To identify additional resources whose expertise is not represented • To ensure that the entire project team (core and extended members) begins to work on the project from the same baseline	• Finalized business case • Finalized project charter • Proposed baseline project timeline • Project background presentation materials (to provide history and background on work done to date) • List of potential subteams and suggested team members	• Confirmed list of core and extended project team members • List of additional resources needed to join the effort due to special expertise or the area they represent • List of newly identified assumptions, constraints, dependencies • List of concerns and issues, with proposed timeline • Draft of subteam groups and team members	• Facilitator • Project sponsor(s) • Project manager • Product manager • Subteam owner(s) • Line of business stakeholder(s) • Marketing representative(s) • Technology representative(s) • Quality professional(s) • Legal representative(s) • Compliance representative(s) • Subject matter expert(s)

(continued)

TABLE 6.1 *(continued)*

Project Meeting	Type or Purpose	This Meeting Is Designed to	Objectives	Inputs	Outputs	Suggested Participants
Lessons learned meetings	Creative development	Gather best practices and identify suggestions for improving the project process. These meetings should be held multiple times throughout the project lifecycle. Provides an opportunity to prioritize and to develop an action plan for implementing the suggested improvements.	• To share best practices • To identify processes that work well • To identify suggestions or ways to improve the process • To discuss impacts of the lesson learned (on people, process, technology) • To identify and prioritize a list of mitigation strategies (that will improve the process for the next project or the next phase) • To identify the owner and a target due date for any improvement activities	• List of individual ideas and thoughts (if participants were asked to provide a sample list prior to the meeting) • List of high-level predefined categories to spark conversation • Lessons learned from previous project efforts that may be applied to this project	• Lessons learned matrix • Mitigation approach	• Facilitator • Project sponsor(s) • Project manager • Project management office representative(s) • Product manager • Subteam owner(s) • Line of business stakeholder(s) • Marketing representative(s) • Technology representative(s) • Quality professional(s) • Legal representative(s) • Compliance representative(s) • Subject matter expert(s)

Project Planning Meetings

This series of meetings allows the project manager to work with the core project team to begin creating the road map for success discussed previously. Based on the finalized project charter, they will build a plan, identify potential subteams, and align resources to the overall purpose and scope of the effort.

During these meetings it is imperative that you, the PMF, begin capturing lessons learned and risks as they are mentioned. These items will be accumulated from this and other meetings, then carried forward into the lessons learned meeting at the end of this phase and the risk identification meetings (see Chapter Seven) that occur in the execute phase of the project.

Project Planning Meeting Participants

Because the project planning meetings involve just the core team, the meeting size will be smaller, usually five to seven people. These participants will be responsible for drafting outputs that will ultimately be presented at the project kickoff meeting.

Project Planning Meeting Inputs and Outputs

These meetings translate the project charter into a road map to guide your work. So you'll need the approved charter, along with any other relevant notes or documents, to start the planning effort. Over the course of these meetings you'll develop a high-level project plan or road map, complete with project team members and potential subteam breakouts. You'll also create the kickoff meeting agenda and any presentation or supporting materials needed to communicate the road map.

Project Planning Standard Agenda

Planning meetings are typically one- to two-hour events, each with a specific goal. The frequency of these meetings can vary based on the target timeframe for your project kickoff meeting. If the timeline is aggressive, you may hold multiple planning meetings in a week; if less so, perhaps only one. The following topics are usually discussed at some point during these meetings:

- The high-level road map for the project
- Recommended resources for the work
- What must be done in preparation for project kickoff
- Kickoff meeting attendees and agenda

Project Planning: Face-to-Face or Virtual?

The project planning meetings can easily be conducted virtually. They involve a small number of participants and tend to be largely discussion and information exchange. As for any virtual meeting, agendas should be developed and communicated several days in advance to allow team members the opportunity to prepare.

The Key Deliverable Planning Meeting

The key deliverable planning meeting provides a forum for the project team to discuss and agree on a list of all of the non-negotiable key deliverables required for the effort, the required format of those deliverables, and the owner or team lead responsible for completing each of the agreed-upon deliverables. They can even start to identify interdependencies among deliverables, which will be confirmed during the project timeline meeting.

It's often assumed that this information is understood by all project team members. Unfortunately this is not always (or even typically) the case. Some project team members, even if they have worked for the same organization for years, may not have been exposed to the project methodology being used. So this meeting tends to spark a lot of discussion and uncover a number of questions that would otherwise go undiscovered until late (often too late) in the project. Reviewing the key deliverables can also eliminate the finger-pointing that often undermines the best of project teams because it was not clearly understood who was responsible for or "owned" each deliverable.

Project teams that take the time to hold a key deliverable planning meeting spend less time scrambling to create project deliverables on the fly because no one understood what was required. If you've ever experienced the futile effort of rehashing the same work over and over because it was not documented in the "standard project format" the first time around, you'll appreciate the value of the key deliverable planning meeting.

Key Deliverable Planning Meeting Participants

This meeting should be limited to no more than twelve people who can speak to the work that must be produced throughout the project. To have a full understanding of the deliverables needed for this project, they should feel free to elicit input from other stakeholders and potential team members prior to the meeting.

Key Deliverable Planning Meeting Inputs and Outputs

It's really helpful to come to this meeting with a list of standard project deliverables, if one exists, or a list from a similar type of project. If you have templates for these deliverables, you should bring them as samples. You'll also want to know the subteams and subteam members identified during your planning meetings and their associated roles and responsibilities.

Your goal is to leave the meeting with a list of nonnegotiable key deliverables, their agreed-upon formats, and their owners. Some of these deliverables will require additional collaborative meetings during the execute phase of the project (such as business requirements, technical design, implementation approach, and so on), so you'll want to identify the target completion dates for these deliverables in preparation for your timeline creation meeting.

Key Deliverable Planning Standard Agenda

Allow at least two hours for the key deliverable planning meeting. From that experience you'll be able to tell whether an additional meeting is needed to complete the task or if you can follow up individually to finalize the list. A typical agenda includes

- *Roll call.* The names of all participants and the areas they represent.

- *Define deliverables.* Review the list of potential deliverables and identify which are necessary for this project. Discuss whether there are standard formats or templates that should be used and determine if any nonstandard or missing deliverables are required. If there is a program or project office that oversees project efforts in your organization, check with representatives from those areas to ensure that any special requirements they may have regarding deliverables are being met. Also discuss which of these deliverables require collaborative meetings.

- *Define owners.* Determine which subteam or organization is responsible for the various deliverables.

- *Review outstanding issues.* Review any issues, risks, or assumptions identified during the discussion and determine whether action items are required for follow-up.

Key Deliverable Planning: Face-to-Face or Virtual?

The key deliverable planning meeting can be conducted virtually even though it's considered a creative development meeting. It involves a small number of participants and requires no special visual aids. However, any time you are determining whether to hold a meeting face-to-face or virtually, you must consider variables such as the following:

- Meeting type
- Meeting objectives

- Number of participants
- Cost
- Location and availability of meeting space
- Collaborative tools you have available for use

As you can see, there is no cookie-cutter approach. You will need to evaluate each meeting prior to making your final decision about how to conduct it.

The Timeline Creation Meeting

The timeline creation meeting can be either a stand-alone meeting or addressed as an activity in the framework of the kickoff meeting. However, if time allows, we suggest you hold it as a stand-alone meeting. Focusing on the timeline always proves to be an exciting experience and uncovers many hidden assumptions and interdependencies. And a stand-alone timeline meeting generally produces a more realistic view of the tasks and deadlines that must be met. Often the output from a stand-alone meeting is better than when it's forced into a limited timeframe in another meeting.

As in the project planning meetings, risks and lessons learned may come up as a natural part of the discussion. When they do, you need to capture them for use in the lessons learned meeting at the end of this phase and the risk identification meetings (see Chapter Seven) that occur in the execute phase of the project.

Timeline Creation Meeting Participants

As we discussed in Chapter Five, engaging the right participants is essential to the success of the meeting and ultimately the project as a whole. But it's just as important to have the right number of people at the table as it is to ensure that the *right* people are present. Timeline creation requires that you pay critical attention to both. This meeting may require more than twelve participants to get a true representation of the voices that need to be heard. See Table 6.1 for a list of recommended participants.

Timeline Creation Meeting Inputs and Outputs

As input to the timeline discussion, you'll want to gather any relevant product, system, or application release or blackout dates, the list of project deliverables, and your project road map. These will all be used to map out the next layer of detail around milestones and dates. As a result of this meeting you'll have an agreed-upon project milestone timeline, along with rationale, outstanding concerns, and related assumptions, constraints, and dependencies.

Timeline Creation Standard Agenda

Developing a milestone timeline and allowing for discussion of interdependencies can take anywhere from two to four hours. The agenda is pretty straightforward and includes the following topics:

- *Roll call.* The names of all participants and the areas they represent.
- *Identification of the milestones.* This is a brainstorm activity involving the placement of the key tasks, deliverables, and known constraints on the timeline.
- *Understanding of dependencies.* Take the time to discuss what tasks are dependent on each other and rearrange the milestones accordingly.
- *Definition of duration and responsible parties.* Once the order of activities has been set, you're ready to define duration and owners. These owners are not individuals but subteams or organizations. Feel free to get creative and use colored dots to depict the various owners.
- *Review of issues and concerns.* At the end of the meeting, take some time to review the issues, assumptions, and risks that have been discussed. Make sure everyone knows what will be done with each item.

We like to visually display the timeline on the wall as we build it, using string and sticky notes to depict time and milestones. You can even vary the colors of the sticky notes to depict whether it's a system constraint, deliverable, or activity. You can also annotate each item to include duration and responsible party, if desired. After the meeting, this visual picture can be reproduced in Microsoft Visio or Microsoft PowerPoint or transcribed into your project planning software.

Timeline Creation: Face-to-Face or Virtual?

This meeting is best held as a face-to-face session. It involves large numbers of participants and collaborative techniques such as brainstorming and visual displays that make it generally more productive if held face-to-face.

Can you get the same results from holding these meetings virtually? Sure. But it will probably take twice as long. You'll need to factor time into your agenda to get your web-based collaboration tool set up, get team members comfortable with it, and actually allow them to use it when actively participating. And because it is often difficult to display all of the components of a timeline on one computer screen, you'll be doing quite a bit of jumping back and forth between screens to refresh people's memories.

The Project Kickoff Meeting

You're now ready to hold the project kickoff meeting. Regardless of the size of a project, this meeting serves as the official beginning of the project and is the first of many that involve the core and extended project team members. We've seen many project kickoff meetings, but the good ones always have the following elements in common:

- *They are well planned.* Not a last-minute convergence, but an orchestrated event that has been thought through. Presentations have been prepared and reviewed by the core team in advance. Everyone knows the order of presentation and how much time they have. Larger events may even have a moderator and timekeeper to keep presenters on track.

- *They are designed from the audience perspective.* The planners have repeatedly asked the question, "What does our audience need to know, and why?" This shift in focus prevents a lengthy, unstructured presentation of data and instead addresses information that will be relevant to team members in order to move forward.

- *They are interactive.* They provide opportunities for getting to know each other, getting questions answered, and discussing key points. They strive for mutual understanding around the project and its road map.

- *They start getting work done.* Good project kickoffs are more than informational. They actually begin the work of the project. We've seen people bring their calendars to start scheduling project meetings. Some project managers allot time for their subteams to meet and begin task planning. And as mentioned before, you can spend time reviewing and validating the timeline. All of these things engage the participants in actually beginning the work of the project.

Project Kickoff Meeting Participants

We have stated that, as a general rule, the number of meeting participants should be limited to between eight and twelve people. But the kickoff meeting is an exception to this rule. Depending on the size of your organization and the size and complexity of the project, you could easily have twenty or more participants.

If you find yourself in this situation, consider adding a second PMF. A second project meeting facilitator allows one to focus on the complex group dynamics while the other focuses on documentation—ensuring that the proper level of detail and information is captured. The last thing you want is to hold a productive meeting, discuss lots of good ideas, and not have any of it documented—or worse, have the outputs documented in such a manner that they are useless when you review them several days later. By dividing the responsibilities between two facilitators, you can ensure a productive meeting that produces useful outputs even with larger numbers of attendees.

You may be asking, "So now where do I find this other PMF when we're already strapped for resources?" Get creative. Pair up with a peer to work as co-PMFs. Your peer can attend your meetings and assist in the documenter role; then you, in turn, can attend their meetings and do likewise. If demanding project responsibilities and time constraints prevent you from pairing up with a peer, check out the other creative ideas listed in Chapter One.

If you can find no other alternative, it may be time to consider hiring outside facilitators. Bringing outside, neutral facilitators to the table allows you as the project manager to actually participate in the meeting and focus solely on your project management responsibilities.

Project Kickoff Meeting Inputs and Outputs

The project planning, timeline, and key deliverables meetings are all held in preparation for the kickoff. Their outputs, along with the approved business case and project charter, serve as inputs to the information presented.

As shown in Table 6.1, the meeting will result in confirmation of the project team and subteams, and the newly identified concerns, issues, assumptions, constraints, and dependencies that result from discussion. In addition, the team will walk away with a shared understanding of the project, its purpose and status, and the folks involved.

Project Kickoff Standard Agenda

The duration of kickoff meetings varies widely. There is no standard. We've seen kickoff meetings that lasted two days because the team was engaged in producing work products, and we've seen kickoff meetings that lasted two hours. Often the duration is linked to whether people are traveling to participate. Project managers will often plan several days of activities by using as much time as possible for the team to work together to justify the travel costs. Typical agenda topics for the kickoff meeting include the following:

- *Welcome and roll call.* Thank everyone for their interest and willing participation. Make sure everyone is introduced by name and the organization they represent.

- *An icebreaker.* Some activity that gets individuals involved with each other on a personal level.

- *The business need.* An overview of why we're doing this project now and what it's intended to accomplish. This may include background research or data that proves the business case and makes the need clear.

- *Project overview.* A discussion of what's been done to date, what's known, what's unknown, and what decisions have already been made. This can include a presentation of
  - Project scope
  - Review of the project subteams
  - Review of key deliverables
  - Preliminary discussion around the project timeline

- *Review of questions and issues.* During the meeting, various questions and issues will be raised. Some of these questions you'll be able to answer; others are unknown. Both types should be captured and reviewed at the end of the meeting. The purpose is twofold: to start building a list of Frequently Asked Questions that can assist in project communication and to identify issues that need escalation to move forward.

- *Project work.* If you're going to engage the team in any special subteam or task work, you'll excuse any unnecessary people at this point and move into work mode.

Project Kickoff: Face-to-Face or Virtual?

There are certain meetings that simply produce better results when held face-to-face; the kickoff meeting is one of them. There are those who would argue that because the meeting is mostly an information exchange, involving a number of presentations, it could be held virtually. In some respects this is true. However, the kickoff meeting is one of the few times, especially if the project team is geographically dispersed, when all of the team members can meet each other.

One of the objectives of the kickoff meeting, as listed in Table 6.1, is to ensure that the entire project team begins to work from the same baseline. But this meeting is as much about team building, putting faces with names, and simply allowing the project team to get to know one another on a personal as well as professional level as it is about setting the stage for all future work. Don't underestimate the power of holding a face-to-face kickoff meeting.

The Lessons Learned Meeting

The lessons learned meeting allows the team to identify best practices and suggestions for improving the project process. The intention is to learn from each other and apply those learnings to the current project and any other projects team members may be involved in. These meetings are often held at the end of a project. But our experience has shown that they're much more valuable when held at the end of each phase, while the tough times and resulting lessons are still fresh in everyone's mind.

Lessons Learned Meeting Participants

These meetings involve a large number of participants to obtain the maximum number of best practices and thoughts on ways to improve the process. So, as mentioned in the project kickoff meeting discussion, you may want to engage a second PMF to assist in managing the meeting documentation so you can focus on the group dynamics.

Lessons Learned Meeting Inputs and Outputs

This meeting works best if you can ask participants to provide their input prior to the meeting. Combine their input with any items captured in prior meetings into one consolidated document and have this ready for the meeting. You'll also want to have an idea of some predefined categories to spark conversation, if needed. The result of this meeting is a set of lessons learned with ideas about how they can be mitigated for future phases and future projects.

Lessons Learned Standard Agenda

Try to keep the lessons learned meetings to two hours or less. Because these meetings will be repeated at each phase, they need to provide a positive experience to promote continued participation. The agenda should include the following topics:

- *Roll call.* The name of each person and the area they represent.

- *Review lessons learned.* If people provided experiences or stories, get the team to translate them into a lesson and discuss the impacts of the lesson on the people, processes, and technology involved. Also review any lessons learned that may exist from previous relevant projects. These can provide a wealth of information to your project team, guiding them in what to do and what to avoid to be successful.

- *Prioritize the lessons.* Determine which ones will affect this project's moving forward and deal with them first.

- *Define mitigation strategies.* For those identified as highest priority, determine how the process can be improved so that the lesson doesn't affect future phases.

- *Define next steps.* Identify the owner and a target due date for any improvement activities.

Lessons Learned: Face-to-Face or Virtual?

The lessons learned meeting can be a successful virtual meeting even though it may involve a large number of participants.

Typically, creative development meetings are best held face-to-face, as suggested in Chapter Five. But to gain maximum benefit from this type of meeting, it should be held at the end of each phase of the project. So we need to be realistic. When working in large, geographically dispersed organizations, it's unlikely that you'll be able to fly participants in from across the country every time you hold a lessons learned meeting. This means that as the PMF, you'll need to get creative about gathering input. For example, send out a Lessons Learned Template and ask the participants to fill in their thoughts in advance of the meeting (see the website for a sample Lessons Learned Template). That way you won't spend additional time on the phone asking for thoughts but instead will be able to use the time reviewing and discussing them.

We have seen this type of meeting work quite successfully with a team of as many as twenty-five people. The project manager consolidated the input into one document and categorized the items prior to the meeting. Then, as one of the first meeting activities, the PMF got them to prioritize the categories. This allowed the team to focus on the highest-priority items and figure out how to best learn from the lessons.

Another creative option is use of a collaborative meeting software tool, such as GroupSystems or WebIQ, which allows team members to type and view ideas in real time. Once the brainstorming is complete, the PMF can walk through the results, holding a brief discussion on each item submitted. When the meeting is over, you'll have a consolidated, updated lessons learned document that can then be carried forward into the next project phase.

Troubleshooting Guide

What Works and What Doesn't Work

Let's take a look at what works and what doesn't work in some of the plan phase meetings. Table 6.2 describes some of the learnings we have found to work well in certain meeting settings.

TABLE 6.2

Plan Phase Meetings: What Works and What Doesn't Work

Project Meeting	Type or Purpose	What Works	What Doesn't Work
Project planning meetings	Creative development	<ul><li>Discussing key roles needed to support the project rather than discussing specific individuals</li><li>Allowing participants to brainstorm about the kickoff meeting agenda rather than trying to develop the agenda from a standard outline</li><li>Reminding participants that these meetings are working meetings and that the outputs still have to be confirmed and agreed to in the kickoff meeting</li></ul>	<ul><li>Forcing a group to identify key resources before individual roles are clearly understood</li><li>Including too many participants too early in the process</li></ul>
Key deliverable planning meeting	Creative development and decision making	<ul><li>Obtaining copies of standard templates used within the organization for certain deliverables</li><li>Including a project management office (PMO) representative to inform the team of required PMO deliverables</li><li>Creating a list of all potential deliverables (both those thought to be nonnegotiable and those thought to be optional) to use as a starting point for discussion</li></ul>	<ul><li>Starting a discussion without reviewing templates used on previous projects</li><li>Failing to consult lessons learned and best practice lists from similar project efforts</li><li>Failing to stay within the defined project scope</li></ul>
Timeline creation meeting	Creative development	<ul><li>Holding this meeting as a stand-alone meeting rather than an agenda item as part of another project meeting</li><li>Allowing adequate time for participants to brainstorm, organize, and rethink key milestone dates</li><li>Revisiting the "finished" timeline by reviewing a second time to determine what tasks can be shortened in duration or done concurrently to reduce the project duration</li></ul>	<ul><li>Creating a timeline without considering key blackout dates (such as holidays, coding, and release freeze periods)</li><li>Failing to overlay the project timeline with key enterprise release dates to identify potential conflicts</li></ul>

TABLE 6.2

Project Meeting	Type or Purpose	What Works	What Doesn't Work
Kickoff meeting	Information exchange	• Holding the meeting face-to-face • Setting aside a portion of the agenda to focus only on team building • Presenting outputs from the project planning, key deliverable planning, and timeline creation meetings to help bring focus to the meeting • Organize the agenda in a logical order—providing background details, then suggested subteams, then proposed timeline, and so on • Capturing additional concerns and issues raised by team members hearing about the effort for the first tlme	• Trying to conduct this meeting virtually without some type of collaboration tool • Assuming all participants have as much knowledge about the project as the core team • Assuming that the participants have taken the time to become familiar with all premeeting materials sent to them
Lessons learned meetings	Creative development	• Providing a standard lessons learned matrix to the team ahead of time • Gathering participant input prior to the meeting • Bringing in lessons learned from previous efforts • Allowing all voices to be heard—a great way to get an open, honest exchange of ideas	• Starting the meetings with a blank document • Re-creating the wheel—not leveraging reference materials, when available, from similar projects on how certain issues were handled

During the plan phase of the project, there are several key things to do—and several to avoid:

- *Do* manage the number of meeting participants. Having too many participants can impede your ability to achieve the meeting objectives.

- *Do* create a free and open environment for your participants to express their ideas.

- *Don't* hold a virtual meeting just because your organization has invested in the latest collaboration tool in the marketplace. Instead, take the time to analyze the best method for conducting your meeting—virtually or face-to-face—depending on its objective.
- *Don't* forget the value of planning and its impact on the rest of your project. So hold off on requirements building until you've got a road map to follow.

Troubleshooting

In Table 6.3 you will find a list of some common problems that arise when facilitating planning meetings. We have outlined the problem and offer some possible solutions to assist in overcoming these problems.

TABLE 6.3

Troubleshooting Guide for Plan Phase Meetings

Problem	Possible Solutions
We have so many resource constraints in my organization—what do I do if I am not sure what resources will be available to support my project?	• Don't let the potential lack of resources at this stage paralyze your ability to move forward. During the project planning meetings, note those possible constraints but still add them to your list of needed resources. The goal is to identify all the resources that you *will need* in order to successfully implement the effort. • Use the scope information found in the project charter to assist in determining what areas need to be represented. • Providing a list of required resources to executives and key stakeholders can be a powerful tool to demonstrate the overall cost and numbers of individuals needed to support an effort. • Solicit the assistance of your sponsors to identify and make the right resources available to the project effort.
I can't get a program management office (PMO) representative to agree to attend the key deliverable planning meeting; what should I do?	• Hold the key deliverable planning meeting. Get the working team to agree on the key deliverables, the formats, and what is considered by the project team to be nonnegotiable. Once the output of the meeting is documented, request that the PMO representative review the documentation and add any PMO-specific requirements. Once the final version is consolidated and agreed upon, it should be ready to use as an input to the kickoff meeting. However, if the PMO in your organization generally has a set of specific requirements for project teams, attempt to obtain those requirements prior to holding the key deliverable planning meeting. This should help prevent rework later in the planning phase.
I failed to capture lessons learned as they were raised during previous meetings. Now I am at the end of the plan phase and I don't have anything documented. What do I do?	• Send out a Lessons Learned Template to team members that have taken part in any meetings held up to this point and ask for their input by having them complete as much of the template as possible. Consolidate all of the feedback and use that as the starting point for your first official lessons learned meeting.
	(continued)

TABLE 6.3 *(continued)*

Problem	Possible Solutions
No one will agree to attend the key deliverable planning meeting—some say it is a waste of time because they have been working on project teams in the organization for years. They ask, "What could be so different about this project effort?" What can I do to encourage them to attend?	• Every project is different, even if the same or similar deliverables need to be built. Often project methodologies have both mandatory and optional deliverables, depending on project scope or complexity. This meeting is essential to agree upon what must be delivered in this project situation. • Ask your executive or project sponsor to send out the invitation, stressing the importance of this foundational meeting. Ask the executive or sponsor to open the meeting and explain the importance of confirming what key deliverables must be completed in order to be successful. It is amazing how many people will clear their calendars when a person with critical influence originates the invitation.
I can't afford, from a budget standpoint, to bring everyone together for a face-to-face timeline creation meeting. I'm not sure this will work virtually. Can it be done?	• Yes. But it will require a very structured agenda and generally works best when done over the course of several meetings that are limited in duration to one or two hours. Ask participants to submit key milestones prior to the beginning of the meeting to be used as a baseline. Then focus each meeting block of time on one topic, for example: • First meeting: Review identified milestones (add and delete as appropriate). • Second meeting: Identify dependencies. • Third meeting: Review duration of each activity; compress activity duration when able. • Fourth meeting: Finalize the proposed timeline and capture any outstanding questions, issues, or known constraints. If working virtually, use appropriate meeting technology to support making the effort as visual as possible.

TABLE 6.3

Problem	Possible Solutions
My manager has demanded that I hold a kickoff event immediately. I have been told there is no time to hold a project planning, key deliverable planning, or timeline meeting prior to the kickoff meeting. Even after explaining the importance holding the individual meetings prior to the kickoff, I was told to "just make it happen." What can I do?	In situations like this, the meeting quickly becomes a working session instead of an information-exchange meeting. Some tips to help increase the chances of it being successful: • Insist that the meeting be longer than one day in duration. Generally, three days is a good rule of thumb. Set the expectation up front that the outputs will not be at the same level of detail as they would have had the planning meetings been held individually. • Gather as much as possible of the background material that would have been input into the project planning, key deliverable planning, and timeline creation meetings. • Develop a list of attendees based on the information you have (use the project charter as a starting point). If you are questioning whether representatives of one area will be affected, invite them. If time allows, place a courtesy call to those representatives you are unsure of, provide a high-level overview of the effort, and ask them if it sounds like something that would affect them. • Create an agenda that incorporates the elements of all of the meetings mentioned in the plan phase—establish a time to work on the initial planning of resources and focus on roles and responsibilities, key deliverable planning, and project timeline. • Have project team members break into small teams to work on what would normally be done in the individual plan phase meetings. • Bring the groups back together to review each activity and agree on outputs before moving forward to the next agenda item. • The creation of what would normally have been presented in the kickoff meeting is actually being developed in this type of kickoff work session setting.

Chapter 7

Facilitating Project Execution Meetings

It's important to know that words don't move mountains.
Work, exacting work moves mountains.

—DANILO DOLCI (1924–1997)

WOW! THE NEW DEVELOPMENT PROJECT Joe inherited has come a long way since he was asked to take over as project manager. It's now time to execute the road map created in the plan phase of the project. Because he took the time to step back, plan the effort, and gain consensus on the purpose, objectives, and scope, he should now have everything he needs to begin the execute phase.

The execute phase is filled with obstacles—some expected (based on anticipated risks) and others not—that will test every ounce of leadership and facilitation skills he has. How these roadblocks are handled will play a big part in the overall success of the project. Despite all the hard work and planning that has taken place, even a project that appears to be healthy and tracking toward a successful completion can unravel quickly if not adequately executed.

Overview of the Execute Phase

During the execute phase of the project you'll be completing the work defined in the project management plan, with the goal of accomplishing the project's objectives, as defined in the project scope statement (PMI, 2004). This is the stage when the work actually is being done. To achieve this goal and provide the necessary supporting communications, we'll be initiating eight new meetings and holding another lessons learned meeting (see Chapter Six). Figure 7.1 shows each meeting and its relationship to the other meetings in this phase.

FIGURE 7.1

Execute Phase: The Project Meeting Road Map

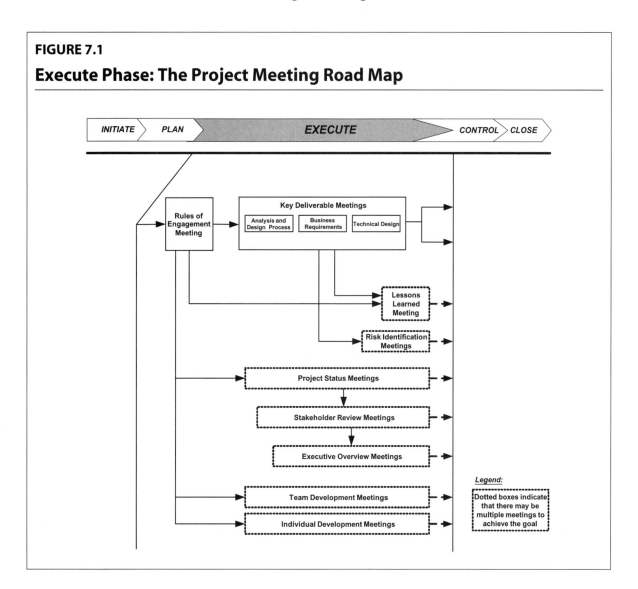

Project Execution Meetings

The eight new meetings introduced in this phase will aid in developing the project team, planning and designing the work, avoiding obstacles, and communicating progress.

Two of these meetings—the rules of engagement meeting and the key deliverable meetings—*occur only in this phase* of the project. But the other six meetings will *start in this phase and continue throughout subsequent phases* of the project:

- Project status meetings
- Stakeholder review meetings
- Executive overview meetings
- Risk identification meetings
- Team development meetings
- Individual development meetings

Table 7.1 provides an overview of each of these meetings.

Rules of Engagement Meeting

The rules of engagement meeting is all about how the team will work together. During this meeting you'll get agreement on the team meeting schedule, team member roles and responsibilities, status reporting process and guidelines, escalation guidelines, and how to access project documentation. This gives the team a framework for how project communication and documentation will be handled during the course of the project.

Rules of Engagement Meeting Participants

Because the rules of engagement focus on the core project team, the number of people involved typically ranges from between five and ten. However, the results of this meeting—specifically, status reporting processes (frequency, due dates, format, and recipients) and how to access project documentation—will need to be shared with the extended team.

TABLE 7.1

Execute Phase Project Meetings

Project Meeting	Type or Purpose	This Meeting Is Designed to	Objectives	Inputs	Outputs	Suggested Participants
Rules of engagement	Decision making	Bring the members of the newly formed project team (core and extended) together to agree on the approach of how project documentation and communication will be handled during the course of the life of the project. This includes determining the standing meeting schedule, the roles and responsibilities of each team member, status reporting guidelines, escalation guidelines, and where and how to access project documentation.	• To clarify the roles and responsibilities of each team member • To establish the status reporting guidelines (frequency, due dates, format, recipients) • To establish escalation guidelines (document severity levels, key contacts, and methods of communication) • To identify where project documentation will be stored • To outline overall project communication processes • To schedule a standing project meeting (day, time, frequency)	• Confirmed list of core and extended project team members • Preliminary list of potential project roles (outputs from planning meetings) • Draft of subteam groups and team members • Output from project planning and kickoff meetings	• Roles and responsibilities matrix (RACI chart: R = Responsible, A = Accountable, C = Consulted, I = Informed) • Scheduled standing project meetings • Finalized list of subteams and subteam members • Scheduled subteam meetings • Status reporting guidelines • Escalation guidelines • Documentation storage process • Communication approach (for project team members)	• PMF • Project manager • Core project team

(continued)

TABLE 7.1 *(continued)*

Project Meeting	Type or Purpose	This Meeting Is Designed to	Objectives	Inputs	Outputs	Suggested Participants

Project status meetings	Information exchange	Provide an opportunity for individual team leaders to give an update on the current status of their progress.	• To provide the status of work completed to date
			• To identify activities that were scheduled but did not occur
			• To provide a status on any open issues
			• To identify issues that will stop forward progress of the effort if not resolved
			• To determine what information needs to be shared in the stakeholder review meeting
				• Individual team member status reports, listing
				  • Accomplishments
				  • Work scheduled but not completed
				  • Issues
				  • "Roadblock" items preventing forward progress until resolved
				  • Next steps
					• Consolidated status report to share with stakeholders
					• List of cross-functional issues and impacts
					• List of "roadblock" items that require stakeholder and executive decisions
					• List of next steps in the project effort
						• PMF
						• Project sponsor(s)
						• Project manager
						• Product manager
						• Project core team
						• Subteam owner(s)
						• Supporting functions such as quality professional(s), legal, and compliance representative(s)
						• Subject matter expert(s)

Project Meeting	Type or Purpose	This Meeting Is Designed to	Objectives	Inputs	Outputs	Suggested Participants
Stakeholder review meetings	Information exchange	Provide status of the progress made to date, outline key issues, and ask for direction to clear roadblocks preventing the project from moving forward.	• To provide current status and health of the project • To outline key risks and issues facing the project team • To escalate issues that require stakeholder input for resolution • To confirm that the project is on track with the overall vision of the stakeholders • To determine what information will be presented in the executive overview meeting	• Consolidated status report (from project status meeting) • List of "roadblock" items that require stakeholder and executive decisions • List of next steps in the project effort	• One-pager • List of stakeholder resolutions to "roadblock" items • List of unresolved "roadblock" issues to escalate to the executives for decision	• Project sponsor(s) • Project manager, PMF • Line of business stakeholder(s)

(continued)

TABLE 7.1 *(continued)*

Project Meeting	Type or Purpose	This Meeting Is Designed to	Objectives	Inputs	Outputs	Suggested Participants
Executive overview meetings	Information exchange	Provide an opportunity for the stakeholders and project manager to meet with the executives to report status of the progress made to date, outline key issues, and ask for direction to clear roadblocks preventing the project from moving forward. It is very similar to the stakeholder review meetings. It is often a smaller audience than the stakeholder meeting (or is a subset of participants). (Refer to the one-pager document described in Chapter Three.)	• To provide current status and health of the project • To confirm that the project is on track with the overall vision of the executive team • To outline key risks and issues facing the project team • To escalate issues that require executive input for resolution	• One-pager • List of unresolved "roadblock" issues to escalate to the executives for decision	• List of executive resolutions to "roadblock" items • List of questions for project team members from executives	• Key executive(s) • Project sponsor(s) • Project manager, PMF • Line of business stakeholders, if required to better understand the issues

Project Meeting	Type or Purpose	This Meeting Is Designed to	Objectives	Inputs	Outputs	Suggested Participants
Risk identification meetings	Creative development	Identify and assess the high-level risks associated with the project. Some areas of focus include (but are not limited to) customer, employee, finance, operation, and market risks. A more in-depth meeting may include identifying all the ways a product or process may fail.	• To identify the potential risks surrounding the project effort • To identify the causes and impacts of those risks • To agree on the required actions and mitigation strategy	• List of risks identified during any of the key deliverable meetings (such as analysis and design meetings, business requirements meetings, technical design, implementation approach, communication approach, training approach) • Any other identified risks from previous project phases	• Prioritized list of risks by severity, probability of occurrence, and detectability • Mitigation strategy for identified risks • Identified "owner" to monitor the mitigation strategy	• PMF • Project sponsor(s) • Project manager • Product manager • Project core team • Subteam owner(s) • Line of business stakeholder(s) • Marketing representative(s) • Technology representative(s) • Quality professional(s) • Legal representative(s) • Compliance representative(s) • Subject matter expert(s)

(continued)

TABLE 7.1 *(continued)*

Project Meeting	Type or Purpose	This Meeting Is Designed to	Objectives	Inputs	Outputs	Suggested Participants
Team develop-ment meetings	Coaching	To encourage the development of a cohesive team and address any roadblocks preventing team members from being effective in their roles.	• To review project goals • To identify ways to improve the group's experience • To assess what is working well • To identify roadblocks that are preventing the project team from moving forward	• Project scope, purpose, objectives • Team member project experiences	• Confirmation that project goals are in alignment with overall business strategy • List of roadblocks that need to be escalated • List of best practices (to be incorporated into the Lessons Learned Matrix)	• PMF • Project sponsor(s) • Project manager • Core and extended project team(s)
Individual develop-ment meetings	Coaching	Review individual interests, set long-term and short-term goals, and establish key developmental steps to ensure continued professional growth.	• To review individual goals • To correlate project team goals with individual goals • To agree on career path steps	• Individuals' goals • Project team's goals • Project manager's goals • Observations regarding individual performance • Any other issues or topics to be discussed	• Career development plan • Action plan for resolution of issues, if any • Commitment to development steps	• Project manager • Individual team member(s)

Rules of Engagement Meeting Inputs and Outputs

Before going into this meeting, you'll need to know your project team—both core and extended—and have a basic grasp of the roles. You'll use the output from the project planning and kickoff meetings as a starting point for discussion.

The goal of this meeting is to create a document outlining the agreements and processes necessary to support the functioning of the project team. The rules of engagement document should become a reference tool that project team members use for the duration of the project. For that reason, the meeting should be designed to answer questions like these:

- What's the best way for us to contact each other?
- When's the best time to meet?
- How often do we need to meet as a core team? As the extended team?
- How do we want to keep each other informed on progress? How often does this need to occur?
- What happens if we can't reach agreement on project issues?
- How should we handle major obstacles that could delay or otherwise affect our portion of the project?
- Where will project information and documentation reside? How does it get there? Who can view or update it?
- What types of information get shared at which meetings? How do the various project update meetings—project status, stakeholder review, and executive overview meetings —differ from each other, and what does that mean to this team?

Some of this discussion may have started during the project planning meetings, but now is the time to formalize it. So, if possible, come in with a draft answer to each of these questions to kick-start discussion.

Rules of Engagement Standard Agenda

As shown in Figure 7.1, this meeting should be the first one you hold after the project kickoff. Plan on two to four hours for discussion and clarification of the various roles and processes. Standard agenda topics include the following:

- Clarifying the roles and responsibilities of each team member
- Establishing the status reporting guidelines (frequency, due dates, format, recipients)
- Establishing escalation guidelines (document severity levels, key contacts, and methods of communication)
- Identifying project documentation processes
- Discussing project communication processes
- Scheduling a standard project meeting (day, time, frequency)

Rules of Engagement: Face-to-Face or Virtual?

This meeting can be held virtually if draft documentation is sent out in advance and collaborative meeting software is used to track changes. Because there are so many different topics to cover, you'll need to keep a tight rein on the conversation and make sure transitions between topics are clear.

Key Deliverable Meetings

The primary portion of the execute phase focuses on creating the project deliverables identified in the plan phase and executing against them (that is, creating the requirements and specs, then building the product). Creating these deliverables may involve meetings to analyze and improve business processes, define requirements, and create various technical designs and plans (such as high-level design, detailed specifications, implementation plans, detailed test plans, marketing campaign). At this point you are executing what was identified in the plan phase during the project planning and key deliverable planning meetings. If the project charter is the foundation of the project, the outputs from these key deliverable meetings are the support beams on which everything else rests. Figure 7.1 groups all of these meetings under the umbrella of key deliverable meetings.

The numerous meetings that fall under the key deliverable umbrella will be far more productive if you limit the number of participants to no more than fifteen. This smaller core group, consisting of participants with the right level of expertise and decision-making authority, will build the deliverables. For many of these deliverables, an additional meeting will be required to get input and approval from a larger extended team. Again, refer to those key participant questions outlined in Chapter Five *every* time you create a list of potential participants and ask yourself if everyone invited is *really* needed for the meeting to be a success (see the website for the Key Participant Checklist).

Because these meetings vary from project to project, we're not going to attempt to cover all the options. In the Resources and References section you will find books that give more detail about the standard participants, objectives, inputs and outputs, and agendas for key deliverable meetings such as process analysis, business requirements, and so on.

Project Status Meetings

This is probably the best known of all project meetings. It provides an opportunity for everyone involved in the effort to stay connected and learn about the work going on in the multiple work streams. However, if not well facilitated, it can also be a boring and unproductive use of the team's precious time. So keep the meetings focused and, whenever possible, inject a bit of fun and humor into the mix. Exhibit 7.1 presents some ideas for this.

Project Status Meeting Participants

The number of people that take part in the project status meetings can become rather large (generally twelve to twenty

---

EXHIBIT 7.1

Did You Know?

Ever experienced one of those necessary but long project status meetings? The ones that seem to go on forever because the project is complex and a number of subteam members must provide weekly updates?

As with many project status meetings, over time a pattern develops: people tend to join, provide their update, and then drop from the conference line or excuse themselves from the meeting. Since this defeats the purpose of sharing information across work streams, one team we recently worked with added a Did You Know? segment to the end of each weekly status meeting. It turned out that the Did You Know? agenda item actually became a much anticipated and requested aspect of the meeting.

Did You Know? takes very little time to pull together and can be great fun. Simply:

- Gather little-known interesting, but innocent, facts about a project team member. Share them with the larger team at the end of the meeting and have all team members guess who was the featured "person of the week." This is a great way to get to know team members.

- For a geographically dispersed team, gather trivia questions from the Internet or other source about countries, states, and cities that are represented in the meeting and ask the team members trivia questions.

- Have team members bring in pictures of themselves when they were younger, send them out with the agenda, and then at the end of the meeting see if anyone can guess who they are.

The Did You Know? segment added some much needed fun and energy to what was a very necessary but often dry meeting. It was also simple and quick to pull together. It turned out to be a great team-building exercise for everyone involved.

---

participants, depending on the number of defined subteam leads). Because this meeting is devoted to providing a status report on the work completed to date, any cross-functional issues, and the escalation of any roadblocks to forward progress, it is imperative that as many members of the core and extended project teams as possible attend.

Project Status Meeting Inputs and Outputs

The goal of this meeting is to understand any issues that might affect other subteams or the progress of the project in general. Accomplishments should also be mentioned and celebrated (for example, we ran the test and got zero defects, or we're two weeks ahead of schedule). Refer to Table 7.1 for a list of the typical inputs and outputs for each of the meetings discussed in this chapter.

Project Status Standard Agenda

Brief is better when it comes to project status meetings. In fact, having more frequent status meetings is better than having longer ones. So shoot for between thirty minutes (for small projects) to two hours (for large projects). Because this is an information exchange meeting, there should not be a great deal of dialogue or discussion of issues—just the presentation of current project status. This needs to be stated clearly at the beginning of each of these meetings to help keep things on track. Issues or varying points of view need to be quickly taken off-line for further discussion.

Developing a well-structured agenda and ensuring that all team members submit their status reports in the same standard format are tasks critical to conducting a productive project status meeting. Standard items to be covered include the following:

- *Roll call.* The names of all participants and the areas they represent.
- *Accomplishments.* List successes since last status update
- *The status of work.* Progress compared to what was originally planned; any unexpected wins or quirks that others should be aware of.
- *Work scheduled but not completed.* Review any items on the work plan that were scheduled to be completed but have not been started or are behind schedule. Provide the reason for the delay and commit to a new target date.
- *Cross-project issues.* Status of any open issues affecting the project and any new issues that may stop forward progress of the effort if not resolved.
- Discuss what information needs to be shared in the stakeholder review meeting.

Project Status: Face-to-Face or Virtual?

This is typically a virtual meeting, because it's focused on information exchange and has such a large number of participants (who could be geographically disbursed around the world). Because status meetings can become so routine, you may want to consider spicing things up by using the tips mentioned in Chapter Three for making virtual meetings more effective.

Stakeholder Review Meetings

This is the second type of status meeting that a project manager must keep in mind. Stakeholder reviews provide a vehicle for keeping stakeholders aware of the progress made to date and key issues affecting the project. They also provide a forum in which the project manager can ask for direction to clear roadblocks preventing the project from moving forward.

In some organizations stakeholders choose to sit in and listen to the regularly scheduled project status meetings. In these cases, an element of the stakeholder review meeting should provide a forum for the stakeholders to ask questions to clarify statuses they heard while attending the project status meeting. Whether the stakeholders attend the project status meeting *and* the stakeholder meeting or wait to hear an update in the stakeholder review meeting, it's important that the first review meetings held with stakeholders establish the right set of objectives, tone, and format so that stakeholders will see them as valuable and continue to engage.

Stakeholder Review Meeting Participants

This meeting is limited to the project manager, sponsor, and stakeholders. Typically the project manager will serve as the PMF for these meetings rather than engaging a separate resource. The number of stakeholders will vary by project depending on the cross-functional impacts of the project.

Stakeholder Review Meeting Inputs and Outputs

The results of the project status meetings serve as inputs to the stakeholder reviews. The goal of this meeting is to determine what actions the stakeholders are going to take to resolve any escalated items and what, if anything, needs to be escalated to executive management. See Table 7.1 for the detailed list of meeting inputs and outputs.

Stakeholder Review Standard Agenda

These meetings are held less frequently than project status meetings. So if you're holding weekly status meetings, you may meet with stakeholders only every other week or maybe even once a month. Some projects we've participated in vary the frequency of these meetings as they go—starting out monthly and ramping up to weekly during the critical weeks of execution. The visibility of the project and the criticality of issues being uncovered will help you determine the best frequency and duration for the meetings.

The primary topics covered at each meeting are

- The current health of the project
- Any key risks or issues that the stakeholders need to be aware of or address
- Any questions or concerns the stakeholders may have
- Determining what information, if any, needs to be presented to executives

Stakeholder Review: Face-to-Face or Virtual?

The stakeholder review meeting is designed to provide a means for information exchange between the project manager and the stakeholders. Due to the international nature of many projects in today's global economy, this type of meeting may have to be virtual. But whenever possible, try to be face-to-face with a small subset of the stakeholders. This will keep your presence known and the discussion lively.

Executive Overview Meetings

The executive review meeting is the third type of status meeting a project manager must consider. Think of it as a steering committee. It provides an opportunity for the project manager and key stakeholders to get guidance, direction, and necessary authorization from the executives sponsoring the project.

Executive Overview Meeting Participants

The number of participants that take part in the executive overview meetings should be an even smaller subset of the stakeholder meetings. So ideally these meetings should consist of no more than three to five participants, because they are truly a forum for the project manager to provide information on the status of the project and to ask for any assistance needed from the executives (see Table 7.1 for suggested participants).

Executive Overview Meeting Inputs and Outputs

The primary input for this meeting is the one-pager (see Chapter Three for a description) and the items escalated by the stakeholders. Although this is considered an information exchange, it also requires decision making. If you leave the meeting without some plan for addressing the issues, the time was wasted. So in your one-pager, focus on defining the costs and impacts of the issue and presenting the alternatives for resolution.

Executive Overview Standard Agenda

Often these meetings are set up on an as-needed basis rather than regularly scheduled. However, if in your organization people's calendars fill up quickly, get permission to hold a two-hour block on the executives' calendar each month to ensure they'll be available if you need them. We suggest establishing a regular, consistent time for these meetings, because in today's fast-paced work environment changes occur so quickly from a project and business perspective that if left unchecked, what once was a common goal can suddenly morph into two different and sometimes contradictory goals. So plan to touch base with the executives on a regular basis.

The topics covered are similar to those addressed by the steering committee and include

- A brief update on the status of the project
- Any key risks or issues the executives need to address
- Validation of the project vision and goals (just to make sure nothing has changed)

Executive Overview: Face-to-Face or Virtual?

These meetings are best held face-to-face. This allows a more personal way of discussing potential landmines and provides the added dimension of reading all those nonverbal cues. However, if this is not possible due to travel schedules or geographical placement, make sure your one-pager contains all the information needed to present an adequate update and list any issues requiring executive input. And as always when working virtually, send the meeting materials in advance. Don't send a one-pager out minutes before the start of the meeting and expect executives to review it in advance. We suggest you send out the materials, along with a meeting reminder, no later than the day before the meeting.

Risk Identification Meetings

Risks are events or issues that might cause a project to fail to meet its intended objectives. Risks might also cause a detrimental customer or business impact. It's necessary to understand the risks associated with a project to determine whether to spend the time, effort, and cost required to mitigate them or to accept them as a necessary risk of doing business (Means and Adams, 2005). This meeting is intended to allow the team to identify and evaluate those risks to determine whether mitigations or contingencies are required. Initial assessment may focus on perceived risks the project poses to customers, market share, revenue, operations, and branding. A more in-depth meeting, held around the time of testing or implementation, may include potential product or process failures and their impact on project success.

Risk Identification Meeting Participants

The meeting participants should include everyone involved in the scope of work being assessed, so the point at which you're holding the risk session will determine who should be invited. For example, you'll have different attendees if assessing risk as part of your requirements than you will during implementation.

Risk Identification Meeting Inputs and Outputs

These meetings are tedious and detailed, so it's best to arrive with a draft of the known risks (identified during any of the key deliverable or other previously held meetings), ready for review by the team. Your goal is to understand which of the risks are most probable and severe and what you'll do to prevent them or minimize them should they occur. These plans need to be documented as part of your risk mitigation strategy.

Risk Identification Standard Agenda

Risk identification meetings may be held several times throughout the execution and control phases. We've seen them occur in conjunction with development of business requirements, again during testing, and often again immediately prior to implementation. We've even seen an initial high-level risk assessment performed during the project charter. Whatever the phase, try to keep them to four hours or less—even if that means convening a subteam to finalize mitigation plans.

The standard agenda includes the following items:

- *Roll call.* The names of all participants and the areas they represent.
- *Set the boundaries.* The goal of this activity is to clearly understand the boundaries of the risk assessment. It may

encompass all segments and phases of the project or it may be focused on specific parts of the implementation.

- *Review known risks.* These are items that have already been captured as a result of ongoing meetings. Get clarity around the nature of the risk and its impacts (how severe, how detectable, and how probable).

- *Identify additional risks.*

- *Discuss how to address high-impact risks.* Develop a mitigation or contingency plan as needed.

- *Determine what, if anything, needs to be communicated to executives.*

For detailed information about risk assessment sessions, see our book *Facilitating the Project Lifecycle* (Means and Adams, 2005).

Risk Identification: Face-to-Face or Virtual?

Risk identification meetings require large numbers of participants to be involved in activities such as brainstorming, in-depth thinking, focused discussion, and accurate capture of ideas and agreements. So these meetings are generally more productive if held face-to-face. As mentioned in Chapter Six, you can get the same results virtually, but you'll need to allow more time and structure the meetings carefully to minimize tangential conversation. If these must be held virtually, you might consider holding smaller, more focused risk sessions followed by a larger group validation session to review and approve the recommended mitigations.

Team Development Meetings

One main aspect of these meetings is team building. They encourage the development of a cohesive team and address any roadblocks preventing team members from being effective in their roles. Use them to discuss communication issues, ways to improve communication across subteams, ways to work better together, concerns about PMO-imposed constraints, and other team-related matters. Unfortunately, these meetings are often an afterthought—especially when so many other meetings are going on at the same time. However, by not holding them you would do a disservice to your greatest asset—the people doing the work.

One project team we worked with held a team development meeting to discuss ways to better communicate across subteams (which had been a huge issue). Afterward they played paint-ball and concluded the day's work with a group dinner. It was a great way to thank the team for all the work done to date and collectively take a break before the final implementation push. Another team met to discuss differences between what the project manager and PMO were requesting around project deliverables. Although the meeting objective was not to resolve the differences, it did provide a forum for the team to discuss and capture the issues so the voice of the employee could be escalated appropriately. The meeting allowed the team to finally be heard and was followed by a team dinner.

By allowing issues to surface and be addressed, you can help prevent internal team issues from festering to the point that the team becomes ineffective.

Team Development Meeting Participants
This meeting is primarily for the core and extended project teams—those who need to interact and communicate to get the work of the project done. Others can be invited to join the subsequent dinner or event, but the discussion of team issues should be limited to the core team.

Team Development Meeting Inputs and Outputs
The formal inputs to these meetings are minimal. The issues are rarely about the project—those things are handled at the project status meetings. Typically, the issues addressed at a team development meeting are interpersonal or organizational. Your goal, as PMF, is to obtain mutual understanding and resolution on issues preventing the team from being successful. If

that's not possible in the meeting, capture the issue and get it addressed through alternate channels (either escalation or one-on-one coaching).

Team Development Standard Agenda

These meetings are a way for teams to come together (sometimes through small events in multiple cities) once or twice during the execute and control phases. Plan some time on the agenda to

- Review the project goals
- Discuss what's working well for the team
- Discuss issues hindering team progress and what can be done about them
- Determine whether any follow-up actions need to occur

But beware—without a focused, structured agenda these meetings can rapidly disintegrate into venting sessions.

Team Development: Face-to-Face or Virtual?

Although you can also conduct the team development meeting virtually, we recommend these meetings be held face-to-face whenever possible. The team development meeting is an opportunity for the project team to review their goals as a whole, discuss the team's overall progress, and allow team members to express concerns about the work environment and anything that may be preventing them from being successful.

If you have to hold this meeting virtually, schedule a conference room at each site so participants at that site can be face-to-face in one room. Because team development meetings are as much about team building as anything else, this is one way to overcome the obstacle of remote locations.

Individual Development Meetings

Working in a project-based environment presents many challenges, but one is the continued growth of the individual. Unfortunately, individual development meetings are often overlooked in the hectic pace of the project environment. Project managers often assume it's the role of the employee's functional manager to provide individual coaching, and the functional managers assume the project manager is coaching the employee to improve performance. After all, in many instances the project manager spends a lot more time with the individual than the functional manager. So who is coaching the employee? Unfortunately, the answer is often "nobody"! As a result, no one takes the time to review individual interests, set long-term and short-term goals, and establish key developmental steps to ensure continued professional growth. To prevent this from happening, as part of the rules of engagement meeting managers should discuss and agree who is the owner of the individual development meetings (see Chapter Six).

You may be asking yourself, "Why would this kind of meeting be included in a book about project meeting facilitators?" Well, on more than one occasion we, as project managers, have found ourselves responsible for conducting individual development meetings, completing individual development plans, and writing performance reviews. This happens more often when the project runs longer than a couple of months, but even for those shorter projects we've found ourselves responsible for employee growth while the project is in flight and for providing written input into the yearly performance review. And why shouldn't we be? The continued development and coaching of our employees is critical for the future success of the organization. So we include this type of meeting for your consideration. It may help you more clearly draw the line between the roles of functional and project managers. And should you find yourself needing to coach a team member, realize that the facilitation skills discussed in Chapters One through Four can apply to individuals just as easily as they do to teams.

Individual Development Meeting Participants

As the title indicates, this is a one-on-one meeting. No team discussions or interventions, just a time for you and the team member to talk about what's important to that individual, his or her personal goals, what's important to you, your suggested goals for the individual, and how the two sometimes opposing perspectives are working together (or not).

Individual Development Meeting Inputs and Outputs

A list of topics to be discussed can be extremely helpful in keeping the meeting focused, so ask folks to think about their personal goals and any other relevant topics prior to coming to the meeting. Don't leave this meeting without a plan for growth. To assist you as you begin to work with your employees, review the GROW method, as discussed in Chapter Four, and apply it when appropriate to individual development meetings.

Individual Development Standard Agenda

If individual development plans were determined to be your responsibility (and not the functional manager's) during the rules of engagement meeting, then you should meet with each project team member on a monthly basis. You may schedule additional meetings as the result of an issue or simply to check in with folks during tough times to see how they're doing. In any case, make sure you have a clear agenda in your mind to guide the conversation. It should include

- Discussing the individual's personal goals
- Discussing performance observations
- Discussing how the personal goals can better align with or complement the project team goals and how the individual can continue to stretch or better enjoy the work being performed
- Determining an action plan; this can focus on resolving a specific issue or steps to career growth
- Obtaining commitment to the action plan steps

Individual Development: Face-to-Face or Virtual?

Because coaching is such a personal thing, we suggest that individual development meetings be held face-to-face whenever possible. The value gained from monitoring those nonverbal cues can be immense. But if time and distance don't make this feasible, you can conduct them virtually.

Many of the facilitation skills discussed in Chapters One through Four can help when working one-on-one with your team members (whether virtually or face-to-face). If you are working with an introverted individual or a detailed thinker and planner, you might share any topics you want to discuss in advance and encourage the person to come to the meeting with a list of prepared questions or goals. Often this makes the employee feel more comfortable, because introverts appreciate having time to process information prior to being put on the spot. Applying facilitation skills to one-on-one encounters can make team members more comfortable and keep the meetings focused.

Execute Phase Recurring Meetings

In Chapter Six we discussed the lessons learned meeting. This is the only meeting from the plan phase that will be conducted again at the end of the execute and control phases (see Figure 7.1). It's natural for the team to talk about lessons they've learned as part of status meetings, team development meetings, and even risk identification meetings. So as you facilitate each meeting, have a blank page ready to capture lessons that can be incorporated into the Lessons Learned Template ahead of time.

Troubleshooting Guide

What Works and What Doesn't Work

Let's take a look at what works and what doesn't work in some of the execute phase meetings. Table 7.2 shows some of the learnings we have found work well in certain meeting settings.

TABLE 7.2

Execute Phase Meetings: What Works and What Doesn't Work

Project Meeting	Type or Purpose	What Works	What Doesn't Work
Rules of engagement	Decision making	• Taking the time to brainstorm all of the possible ways the project team can communicate with one another • Chunking the work into categories for discussion purposes such as communication methods, types and number of standing meetings, standing meeting master calendar events, and documentation standards • Creating a "rules of engagement" template with placeholders that can be completed or added to during the meeting • Continuing to reference the output from the meeting as a reference tool for all team members to consult as needed	• Starting from scratch—not taking into consideration all of the work completed in the plan phase (outputs from project planning, key deliverable, and kickoff meetings) • Trying to rush through discussions on these topics to simply complete a draft
Key deliverable meetings	Creative development and decision making	• Creating drafts of deliverables with a small, core team and then asking for input from the larger team • Overlaying the key deliverable meeting milestones with the timeline created during the timeline creation meeting—ensuring there are no conflicts with dates • Engaging a meeting facilitator who has the skill to not only manage the group dynamics but also translate the input of the group into the appropriate deliverable model • Continuing to cross-check related deliverables to ensure that deliverables created in separate meetings are in sync and not contradictory	• Failing to adhere to the standard document formats agreed to during the key deliverable planning meeting • Allowing the individual key deliverable meetings to consist of more than fifteen participants

(continued)

TABLE 7.2 *(continued)*

Project Meeting	Type or Purpose	What Works	What Doesn't Work
Risk identification meetings	Creative development	• Incorporating risks that have been captured in all other project meetings as input into this meeting • Gathering participant input prior to the meeting • Allowing all voices to be heard—a great way to get an open, honest exchange of ideas • Building contingencies for high-priority risks rather than every risk identified	• Starting the meetings with a blank document • Failure to incorporate risk analysis outcomes into the project plan
Project status meetings	Information exchange	• Having all subteam leads submit their status report using a standard status report template • Consolidating all individual status reports into one document prior to the meeting • Securing conference rooms at each location so participants who are collocated can be in the same room during the meeting • Agreeing on next steps	• Allowing discussion (this is an information-only meeting) • Not including a wide enough audience to hear the latest updates • Allowing participants to multitask during the meeting
Stakeholder review meetings	Information exchange	• Focusing only on overall status and roadblock issues • Allowing stakeholders to ask clarifying questions about items they heard about in the project status meeting (in cases where stakeholders choose to attend project status meetings) • Keeping the presentation materials to a few pages • Holding these meetings face-to-face when possible	• Including too large an audience • Creating too many presentation materials • Trying to rehash the entire project status meeting

TABLE 7.2

Project Meeting	Type or Purpose	What Works	What Doesn't Work
Executive overview meetings	Information exchange	• Creating a one-pager status document (see Chapter Three) • Building time into the agenda for questions—from both the executive and the project manager • Holding these meetings face-to-face when possible • Holding consistent, regularly scheduled meetings to ensure that project and business goals stay aligned	• Including too large an audience • Only holding the meetings when issues need to be resolved
Team development meetings	Coaching	• Creating an environment for participants to express their concerns without fear of repercussions • Focusing on the core team members • Letting the participants have time to vent about frustrations they are experiencing • Being consistent in expressing your expectations of the team	• Holding the meetings on a sporadic basis • Allowing too many participants • Promising to follow up on a group concern and then not doing it
Individual development meetings	Coaching	• Holding these meetings face-to-face when possible • Encouraging participants to come to the meetings with a list of goals, observations of their own performance, and questions prepared in advance • Being consistent in expressing your expectations of the individual • Applying facilitation skills used in larger group settings to individual meetings as appropriate • Obtaining commitment to action steps	• Holding the meetings on a sporadic basis • Promising to follow up on an individual concern and then not doing it

During the execute phase of the project, here are several key things to do or avoid:

- *Do* maintain momentum by taking advantage of the work completed in the plan phase.

- *Do* keep people interested and engaged in project status meetings by incorporating creativity and fun.

- *Do* think about and apply facilitation skills to your one-on-one meetings.

- *Do* hold executive overview meetings regularly to ensure that project and business goals stay aligned.

- *Do* identify who will be responsible for individual team member coaching. If this is not clearly identified at the beginning of the project effort, it is likely to be ignored.

- *Don't* forget about team development. The stages of growth will not happen without your guidance and coaching.

- *Don't* capture issues and concerns in team development meetings and fail to follow up on them.

- *Don't* wait until the lessons learned meeting to identify lessons encountered during this phase. Instead, gather the lessons as a part of each meeting you facilitate.

Troubleshooting

In Table 7.3 you'll find a list of some common problems that arise when facilitating execution meetings and some possible solutions to assist in overcoming them.

TABLE 7.3

Troubleshooting Guide for Execute Phase Meetings

Problem	Possible Solutions
I can only get myself, as the project manager, and my business analyst together to complete the rules of engagement. So can't I just skip this meeting?	• It is not recommended. If only two or three of you can meet, then at least meet and complete a draft of the rules of engagement. • Send the draft to team members for feedback. • Consolidate all feedback into a final draft document. • Review the final draft with the extended team as an agenda item during another standing meeting.
I find that I have multiple people working on the same key deliverable and no one working on others. What should I do?	• Refer back to the outputs from the key deliverable planning meeting. Find out if any of the owners assigned during that meeting have changed. Make updates as needed. • Reconvene the team to review the outputs from the key deliverable planning meeting and take the time to review each deliverable, clarify roles, and publish any updates that result from this meeting to the larger, extended team members.
My project status meetings are beginning to run three hours long, and by the end only a few people are left on the phone to hear the last updates. Things are beginning to fall through the cracks. What can I do?	• First, shorten the meeting duration to no more than two hours. You can do this by providing a very structured "talking points" template outlining what needs to be provided during each individual update. • Speak off-line to individuals that tend to ramble. Coach them on how to provide their updates in concise "bullets" rather than paragraphs of details. • Time-box each individual presenting an update to X minutes. • Reorder the agenda each week so that no one individual is stuck presenting first or last for the duration of the project.
Even though I have a standing executive overview meeting every two weeks, my executive continues to cancel it. How can I get her to meet with me?	• Attempt to find a better meeting time. Call the executive directly or work with the administrative assistant to determine what is the best time to get their attention. • Complete the one-pager (see Chapter Three) and continue to document all issues needing the executive's attention. Forward both the one-pager and the issues list to the executive as you would after a meeting, even if the meeting does not take place. • Follow up with a phone call and email to the executive after you send the one-pager, requesting a call to review the status.

TABLE 7.3 *(continued)*

Problem	Possible Solutions
The functional manager agreed to track and document all items related to my project team member's career development. However, I have recently discovered that nothing has been documented and no meetings are being held. What should I do?	• If it was agreed in the rules of engagement meeting that the functional manager owned the responsibility of individual development, then follow up to find out why the meetings are not taking place. • Provide written feedback to the functional manager on the employee's performance on a regular basis (weekly, monthly) to remind the manager to meet with the employee. • If meetings still don't take place, take it upon yourself to ensure the employee's performance (as it relates to the project effort) is being documented, discussed with the employee, and filed in the employee's permanent personnel file for future reference.

Chapter 8

Facilitating Project Control Meetings

> We cannot direct the wind, but we can adjust the sails.
> —BERTHA CALLOWAY, founder of the Great
> Plains Black Museum

THE GOAL IS IN SIGHT! Joe and his team have made great progress working on the new product development effort and are approaching the final stretch. But now is not the time to let down his guard or get complacent. With all of the hard work and planning behind him, he could take a backseat and let the individual subteam leads begin to execute their plans with little oversight. It's great to allow subteam leads to take ownership and work without micromanagement; however, they must have a standard process to use for evaluating and implementing changes to the original scope of work and handling problem resolution. And establishing this standard process is one of Joe's responsibilities as the project manager.

In addition, Joe must measure progress toward the objectives and take action to ensure that deviations don't adversely affect the end results of the project. This phase will require Joe to apply all he knows about handling unexpected delays, cost overruns, changes in scope, and problem solving (Baker and Baker, 1998).

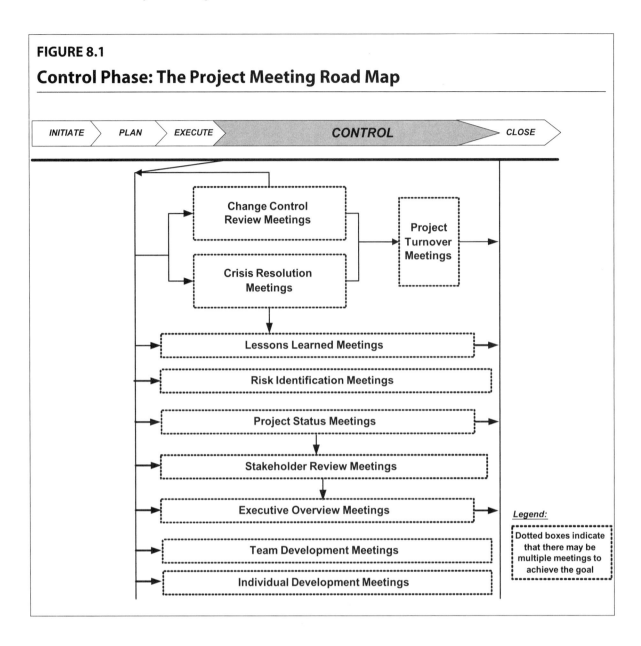

FIGURE 8.1

Control Phase: The Project Meeting Road Map

Overview of the Control Phase

The control phase is all about observing, measuring, and monitoring what's been executed to ensure that it's stable, meets (or exceeds) the original project goals, and is ready for incorporation into the operating practices of the organization (PMI, 2004). To do this, Joe will need to add several new meetings to his already tight schedule. Figure 8.1 depicts where these meetings fall on the project meeting road map.

Project Control Meetings

During this phase, you will continue to hold the recurring meetings mentioned in Chapter Seven, and you'll introduce three new types of meetings: change control meetings, crisis resolution meetings, and project turnover planning meetings. All of these meetings are designed to address obstacles that, left unchecked, could prevent the project objectives from being met. View these meetings as risk mitigation tools. By holding these meetings you'll minimize the chance that the project will derail, and you'll increase the likelihood of delivering it on time, within budget, and according to the original objectives and scope defined in the project charter. Plus you'll ensure that the necessary training and support will be in place to move the project into normal maintenance or operations mode. Table 8.1 provides a description of these meetings.

Unlike the meetings we've discussed in the other phases, the meetings in the control phase do not typically follow a sequential order. So, for example, you may need to conduct a crisis resolution meeting prior to your first change control meeting or vice versa, and these may be interspersed with project turnover planning meetings.

Change Control Meetings

The objectives for change control meetings are to quickly understand the change at hand; to determine effects on the project resources, budget, and timeline; and to arrive at a go-forward approach that does not undermine the original purpose of the effort. To do this, projects need a clear change control process that is embraced and followed by all team members. Change control meetings should follow the change control guidelines that were created in the rules of engagement meeting (see Chapter Seven). Some key outputs are needed from that meeting to support the change control process, such as

- Agreed-upon standard change control request form
- Accessible, centralized location to house the change control request form

TABLE 8.1

Control Phase Project Meetings

Project Meeting	Type or Purpose	This Meeting Is Designed to	Objectives	Inputs	Outputs	Suggested Participants

Change control meetings	Decision making	Review project change control requests, ensuring that the project tracks to the timeline, stays within budget, and does not experience scope creep.	• To review incoming change control requests
			• To provide project team with one of four change control decisions:
			  • Approved
			  • Complete
			  • Deferred
			  • Denied
				• Change control request form	• Decision (approved, complete, deferred, denied) on individual change requests
					• Updated change control matrix
						• Facilitator
						• Project sponsor(s)
						• Project manager
						• Line of business stakeholder(s)

Crisis resolution meetings	Creative development	Gather information when something is not working correctly. The meeting is a brainstorming session in which participants identify the problems, identify ways to correct them, and outline a target timeline to do so.	• To capture key problems and issues faced by the project team • To identify root causes of the problems and issues identified • To identify suggestions to correct the problems and issues • To identify owners of the corrective activities • To agree on a timeline for implementation of the corrective activities • To determine impacts to the overall project timeline	• List of individual ideas and thoughts about the problem (if participants were asked to provide a sample list prior to the meeting) • List of high-level, predefined categories to spark conversation • Project timeline • Risk matrix	• Prioritized list of problems and issues to be resolved • List of corrective activities (with owners and timeframes identified) • Updated project timeline • Updated risk matrix	• Facilitator • Project sponsor(s) • Project manager • Product manager • Subteam owner(s) • Line of business stakeholder(s) • Marketing representative(s) • Technology representative(s) • Quality professional(s) • Legal representative(s)

Project Meeting	Type or Purpose	This Meeting Is Designed to	Objectives	Inputs	Outputs	Suggested Participants
						• Compliance representative(s) • Subject matter expert(s)
Turnover meetings	Decision making	Confirm who is responsible for or owns specific pieces of the project going forward as the effort moves from project status to normal course of business and daily operations. During the meeting, any open action items or issues must have owners assigned and a plan outlined of how to close those items so the project can be officially closed.	• To clearly outline roles and responsibilities of project members to line of business owners • To confirm that all project and implementation issues have been closed • To identify an owner and a timeframe for resolution of any carryover items from the project team to the business owner	• List of open items • List of line of business and daily operations owners	• Proposed roles and responsibilities matrix • List of closed project implementation issues • List of open project implementation issues	• Facilitator • Project sponsor(s) • Project manager • Product manager • Subteam owner(s) • Line of business stakeholder(s) • Marketing representative(s) • Technology representative(s) • Quality professional(s) • Testing representative(s) • Legal representative(s) • Compliance representative(s) • Subject matter expert(s)

- Identification of owner or owners responsible for submitting change control requests
- Deadline for change control request submissions
- Identification of decision makers for all submitted change control requests
- Frequency of change control meetings
- Service level agreement (SLA) about turnaround times from the time a request is submitted until a decision is rendered
- Agreed-upon notification and communication plan for all decisions rendered in the change control meetings

All of these factors are important in creating a productive change control process.

Change controls tend to get a bad rap. The phrase *change control* often conjures up images of project teams scrambling to meet a deadline due to a new set of business or technology requirements or having to find additional testing resources at the last minute. If looked at closely, often the problem with change controls is that a clear process was not built or communicated properly during the plan and execute phases. Some project teams end up spending as much time trying to figure out the process of submitting and getting change controls approved as they do implementing the approved changes, if not more. Or worse, project team members become so frustrated with the lack of a clear change control process that they sidestep whatever sketchy process does exist and begin to implement changes that were never approved. This almost always leads to disaster! Keep in mind that the best-designed processes are of no value if they are not followed.

As you begin to hold change control meetings, remember that not all change controls are negative. Sometimes change controls are submitted and approved because the change could result in a significant cost reduction at implementation or take a shorter time to develop and test.

Armed with the change control guidelines and meeting structure that were designed during the rules of engagement meeting, you should be ready to hold your first change control meeting. It is your responsibility, as the PMF, to ensure that change control meetings are held at regularly scheduled times and that the agreed-upon service level agreements are met.

Change Control Meeting Participants

The change control meeting should consist of a small number of decision-making participants (three to five). These people serve as the change control board, and their participation *should be constant.* Altering the change control board members can introduce a new level of complexity that should be avoided at this stage of the project. Suggested participants include the project manager, the PMF, the project sponsor, and the line of business stakeholders. There are two notable exceptions:

- If the requested change control has significant impacts to the overall project budget, timeline, or number of resources needed, an executive should also be included in discussions before a final decision is made.

- If the requested change control is complex and needs additional background that cannot be easily provided in written documentation, it is suggested that the subteam lead be included in the meeting to provide necessary subject matter expertise.

Change Control Meeting Inputs and Outputs

An increase in change control volume can often be attributed to a significant shift in the original objectives resulting from a fundamental change in the overall business strategy. These strategy changes may also affect the original business requirements. If so, the change control team must determine if the changes can be handled through the change control process or if they are so significant that the original project charter and requirements must be revisited.

Approved change controls may affect a number of the deliverables that were outputs from the individual key deliverable meetings held during the execute phase. The outputs from those key deliverable meetings must also be updated to reflect the changes that have been approved.

Change Control Standard Agenda

These meetings generally range from one to two hours long. But you may need to adjust how often you hold the meeting (frequency) based on the volume of requests. For example, you may begin by holding a change control meeting once every two weeks, then once a week; for large-scale, complex projects you may need to meet every day as the project hits its stride.

The items most often addressed as part of this meeting are:

- *Roll call.* The names of all participants and the areas they represent. Confirm that all participants have the list of changes to be covered.
- *Confirm the number of change control items to be discussed.*
- For each change control request, determine
  - *What is it?* Review a brief description of the change and why it's needed (part of the change control request form).
  - *What will be affected?* Review impacts to resources, budget, timeline, and dependent projects.
  - *What will happen if we don't implement this change?* (Describe best-case and worst-case scenarios.)
  - *What's the decision?* Does the change board agree, reject, or need more information? (See Exhibit 8.1 for explanations of the common decisions.)
- *Wrap-Up.* List all decisions made during the meeting.

Change Control: Face-to-Face or Virtual?

Almost without exception, these meetings tend to be virtual. If you have the luxury of having the project manager, line of business stakeholders, and project sponsor all collocated in the same

---

EXHIBIT 8.1

Change Control Decision Definitions

- *Change control approved.* Change control has been deemed critical to the project and will be implemented prior to the launch of the effort.
- *Change control complete.* Change control has been deemed not critical to the project, but work will begin so that the change can be implemented as soon as possible after the launch of the effort.
- *Change control deferred.* Request for additional information from project team—no decision made on change control request.
- *Change control denied.* Request is not related to the current project and is denied (requires separate business case, funding to be considered as a separate effort outside of the boundaries of the current project).

---

facility, then definitely meet face-to-face. However, in many organizations this is simply not possible. Holding a teleconference is sufficient. Just ensure that all of the participants have access to the change control request forms to be reviewed.

Crisis Resolution Meetings

To prevent the project from getting bogged down by obstacles, you will need to pay special attention as issues surface in these situations, as a crisis resolution meeting may be needed. Because these meetings are held in response to an unexpected issue, they are typically thought of as ad hoc rather than planned meetings. But in spite of their irregular nature, these meetings still have a thoughtful structure. The purpose is to understand the nature of the problem (what isn't working or what roadblock has appeared) and determine a course of action to address it. For example, you may be in the middle of building an application based on the technology requirements, only to discover that a corporate decision to sunset the target application within the next twelve months was made without the knowledge of the project team. Or you may experience the double-posting of financials during a data conversion, causing serious financial implications. In both situations, a crisis resolution meeting should be held to analyze the situation and determine whether to resolve it or adjust course to accommodate it.

The crisis resolution meeting provides a forum to discuss these types of last-minute, unexpected issues and necessary actions, the implications for the budget and timeline, and the overall impacts on your current project as well as other projects that may be dependent on your successful implementation. And though it would be great to never have to hold a crisis resolution meeting, it is highly unlikely that you'll never get the chance. There are always unexpected issues that must be dealt with swiftly.

So now is the time to begin to use some of the outputs you've been building along the way. For instance, you've accumulated lessons learned from both the planning and execute phases. When issues arise, refer back to them to see what's been learned. Also check the lessons learned from previous projects to determine how similar situations were handled in the past.

Each issue that arises during this phase must be resolved quickly. You won't always have the luxury of waiting to have all of the information at your fingertips before making a decision. Sometimes you simply have to go with the information in front of you and make the best educated decision possible—even if this means readjusting your approach once more information becomes available.

Crisis Resolution Meeting Participants
The scope and complexity of the issue that must be discussed determine the number of participants required to take part in the crisis resolution meeting. We suggest you start with a small group of key individuals (five to seven) and, based on the initial discussion, expand the team (to eight to twelve) if a follow-up meeting is necessary. Unlike the change control meetings, the crisis resolution participants do not need to remain constant. The standard core members such as PMF, project manager, and line of business stakeholders generally remain constant, but

beyond that, the additional participants should be limited to those who will bring special expertise to the issue under review. So the list of participants for this type of meeting may vary each time a crisis resolution meeting is convened to discuss a new issue.

Crisis Resolution Meeting Inputs and Outputs

Don't forget to incorporate the outputs from the crisis resolution meeting into your lessons learned and risk identification documents. You may also encounter changes to your project timeline that must be documented and communicated. Refer to Table 8.1 for a list of the typical inputs and outputs.

Crisis Resolution Standard Agenda

Crisis resolution meetings are typically brief. The crisis must be averted, so the focus is on getting a common understanding so appropriate action can be taken. Here is a typical agenda for this type of meeting:

- *Roll call.* The names of all participants and the areas they represent.
- *Define the problem.* Get a clear understanding of the issue or problem and some background around the triggering events.
- *Understand the impact.* What's been affected so far? What will be affected should the problem not be resolved soon? Will any regulatory or legal sanctions be imposed at any point?
- *Make an action plan.* Who is going to do what, and by when? Set a follow-up meeting to check on status and progress.

Crisis Resolution: Face-to-Face or Virtual?

Crisis resolution meetings are, by the nature of their unexpectedness and urgency, almost always virtual. Because this meeting may be called without warning to address a pressing issue, a teleconference is generally the best approach (see Exhibit 8.2). If you have time and there is a reason for using one of the

---

EXHIBIT 8.2

Crisis Resolution Meeting Prep Tip

Identify a teleconference phone line that will be used only for crisis resolution meetings. The telephone number and access code should be determined and published as part of the rules of engagement meeting and subsequent documentation. When a crisis resolution meeting must be held on the spur of the moment to address an emergency issue, identify the key participants, and the only communication that will need to be sent is the starting time of the meeting. All participants, regardless of where they are or what they are doing, should have the dedicated teleconference number and know exactly how to access the secure phone line.

This is a simple tip, but one that, when followed, can save valuable time. Everyone will be able to focus on the issue rather than scrambling to figure out which teleconference number should be used.

---

collaborative tools we have mentioned previously, by all means do so.

Project Turnover Planning Meetings

The project turnover planning meeting is a decision-making meeting designed to identify the key business owners who will be responsible for the daily operation of the newly implemented project and to produce a draft of the formal turnover approach. It is intended to create the framework that will support the transfer of ownership from the project team to the operational line of business owners. This meeting will assist in the identification of any gaps—such as outstanding issues, unfinished project tasks, or items that don't seem to have an operational line of business owner—so that corrective actions can be taken prior to closing the project.

This output becomes a key input into the project wrap-up meeting that occurs during the close phase. Table 8.1 provides a description of the project turnover planning meeting.

Because one of the main objectives of the project turnover planning meeting is to clearly outline the roles and responsibilities as the transition from project to business status unfolds, it can be helpful to remind the project team of the RACI (**R**esponsible, **A**ccountable, **C**onsulted, and **I**nformed) matrix completed during the rules of engagement meeting (see the website for an example of a RACI matrix). You will also be creating a turnover timeline. So take the time to review the objectives you used when holding your timeline creation meeting.

Project Turnover Planning Meeting Participants

The project turnover planning meeting should be of a size that is reasonable for the scope of implementation, but we suggest it consist of fewer than twenty participants. Again, we strongly recommend two project meeting facilitators if there are more than fifteen participants. When attempting to determine the number of participants, don't forget to take into consideration the size of your organization and the size and complexity of the project.

Here's a creative alternative to reduce the size of the meeting and make it easier to handle. You could meet with the core project team first to identify the areas and line of business owners that are thought to be affected. Then, rather than inviting the entire army of participants, invite only those identified in your premeeting analysis. Because you will most likely need to meet with this group repeatedly to develop a clear turnover proposal, you could add or delete members as you learn more from each meeting.

Project Turnover Planning Meeting Inputs and Outputs

It is important for participants to come to project turnover planning meetings well prepared. Because one of the required inputs is a list of any open or outstanding issues or action items, it's best to solicit input from the participants prior to the meeting and take the time to consolidate the list into one master document to work from during the meeting. Other key inputs are an organizational chart or, at a minimum, a list of all of the line of business and daily operation owners and the most current list of all of the project team members originally defined during the rules of engagement meeting.

All of these inputs will be used to generate the primary output of project turnover planning meetings—a draft of the proposed business roles and responsibilities. Any special or unique support or tasks that the project team has been performing will need to be documented and carried forward into the business-as-usual environment.

Last, but by no means of lesser importance, is a consolidated list of all open and closed project issues. As a result of the meeting, this list should reflect the status of all issues—and the open issues should have an owner and agreed-upon due date clearly identified. The closed items on the list will come in handy if a similar issue arises during normal operations. It can be a great reference tool when troubleshooting issues—especially if you are a daily operational owner and this is your first experience with the new application or process.

Project Turnover Planning Standard Agenda

Plan on about two hours for each of these meetings and continue scheduling them until the deliverables have been completed. The items most often addressed as part of this meeting are

- *Roll call.* The names of all participants and the areas they represent.
- *Identify the functions to be operationalized:*
  - Who owns each function?
  - Who is the project team owner?
  - Who is the proposed business owner?
- *Define how the turnover will occur:*
  - Is training required?
  - What is the timing of the turnover? Is this a phased approach?
  - Are there any open items or issues that the line of business owners agrees to accept and resolve?
- *Determine the current status of action items and issues.*

Project Turnover Planning: Face-to-Face or Virtual?

If your project team is collocated, this can be a great face-to-face meeting. You are now so close to the end of the effort that it is a wonderful opportunity for the extended project team to work out the final details together. However, if necessary, the project turnover planning meeting can be conducted virtually. It provides an opportunity for both groups to really appreciate all of the hard work that has gone into implementation. As usual, be aware of the virtual meeting tools and ways to keep a virtual meeting on target, as outlined in Chapter Three.

Control Phase Recurring Meetings

During this phase, you will continue to hold the following meetings introduced during the execute phase:

- Lessons learned
- Risk identification
- Project status
- Stakeholder review
- Executive overview
- Team development
- Individual development

For many project teams, the execute phase provides the last opportunity to formally conduct the individual development meetings. One of the outputs from the last formal individual development meeting should be a developmental document that team members can carry forward with them as they move into their next project roles. This document should be a true reflection of the work they have done while engaged in this effort. Also, keep in mind that any of the individual learnings that the team members want to share with each other should be addressed during the project retrospective meeting (which will be discussed in Chapter Nine).

These recurring meetings continue to be necessary as you strive to ensure that project implementation remains on target and within budget and that the objectives and scope defined in the project charter are fulfilled. But the meeting pace can be hectic. So for project team members, the question becomes, "How do I get my 'real work' done when I am in project meetings all day?" It's time to take a look at how to address meeting frequency and determine "to meet or not to meet?" (see Exhibit 8.3).

Just as the project manager is responsible for constantly evaluating the overall project process, it is the responsibility of the PMF to evaluate the meeting process. Although this is something that should be done in *each* phase of the project, the number of recurring meetings taking place by the time you reach the control phase usually starts to take its toll on project teams. As the PMF, ask yourself the following questions about each type of meeting being held during this phase:

- What was the original purpose of the meeting? Are the objectives still being met?
- What was the original frequency and duration of the meeting? Every day? Twice a week? Once a week? Two hours? One hour?

- Are other meetings taking place with similar objectives? Do those meetings have the same audience? If so, can we consolidate? What are the pros and cons?

- Are the appropriate participants included in the distribution list? Should participants be added or deleted?

- Are the meeting outputs still of value? Are they being used by the intended audience?

If the meeting objectives and outputs are still relevant, then evaluate the meeting frequency (Spivey, 2006). Are you meeting too often? You may have been holding project status meetings twice a week during the execute phase due to the number of interproject dependencies among the numerous subteams. These twice-weekly updates were essential to keeping everyone working in synch. Now that you're in the control phase, you may be able to reduce the frequency to once a week, or perhaps, if things have not gone well, you may need to increase the frequency. This constant evaluation and adjustment of meeting needs will allow your team to apply the extra hours gained toward the main focus—monitoring the execution of the "road map to success" and addressing any roadblocks that may prevent you from a successful implementation.

Troubleshooting Guide

What Works and What Doesn't Work

Let's take a look at what works and what doesn't work in some of the control phase meetings. Table 8.2 provides some words of wisdom.

TABLE 8.2

Control Phase Meetings: What Works and What Doesn't Work

Project Meeting	Type or Purpose	What Works	What Doesn't Work
Change control meetings	Decision making	• Confirming that the correct decision makers will be present when scheduling the recurring change control meetings • Recognizing that not all change controls are negative—many may reduce costs, reduce time to market, improve the overall implementation timeframe • Adhering to the agreed-upon change control process • Being clear on why the change is needed, as well as what will happen if it is not implemented • Adjusting meeting frequency as needed to support the volume of change control requests being received	• Holding change control meetings without a clearly defined and communicated change control process • Altering which meeting participants make up the change control board • Attempting to make decisions about the more complex change requests without including subject matter expert input
Crisis resolution meetings	Creative development	• Keeping the participants to a small number—only including those who are directly impacted or can contribute to the resolution of the issue • Relying on lessons learned and risk mitigation documents to assist in issue resolution • Establishing a unique teleconference number dedicated for the use of all crisis resolution meetings—this eliminates any confusion about where to call when this ad hoc meeting is needed	• Attempting to hold a regularly scheduled crisis resolution meeting to address ongoing issues • Failing to incorporate and document outputs from crisis resolution meetings into appropriate project documentation • Waiting to gather folks together in a face-to-face setting before addressing the immediate issue—even if the project team is collocated
Turnover planning meetings	Decision making	• Including the proper input documents—business as usual and project team roles and responsibilities matrices	• Holding turnover meetings without a list of outstanding issues or action items • Failing to add or delete participants as appropriate when holding multiple iterative turnover planning meetings

Here are several key things to do or to avoid doing during the control phase of the project:

- *Do* avoid unnecessary complexity by keeping the members of the change control board the same throughout the project.
- *Do* monitor the volume of change requests to determine the frequency of change control meetings.
- *Do* approach each crisis resolution meeting with the intention of reaching a decision about what action to take.
- *Do* have all the necessary meeting inputs ready and available to the team before attempting to hold a project turnover meeting.
- *Do* free up as much time as possible for folks to do the work by evaluating whether all the meetings need to continue or occur as frequently.
- *Don't* make modifications to the change control process that are not clearly communicated to *all* project team members.
- *Don't* forget to incorporate the outputs from crisis resolution meetings into the lessons learned and risk identification documents.
- *Don't* reduce your chances of holding a successful meeting by attempting to facilitate too many participants by yourself. If there are more than fifteen people, partner with a skilled colleague.

Troubleshooting

In Table 8.3, you'll find a list of some common problems that arise when facilitating meetings in the control phase and some possible solutions.

TABLE 8.3

Troubleshooting Guide for Control Phase Meetings

Problem	Possible Solutions
What do I do if a member of the change control board accepts a new position and leaves an opening on the board?	• Continue to meet with the remaining team members regularly while a replacement is being identified. Delays in making decisions about change controls can have larger implications for the project timeline, costs, and resources needed to successfully launch an effort. • If possible, identify an interim representative to cover that area until a designated replacement for that board position is found.
I inherited the project in the middle of the execute phase and have discovered that the change control process was not discussed as part of the rules of engagement meeting. Can I just start accepting change control request forms?	• No. The change control process must be documented and communicated to all project team members. If the change control process was not documented as part of the rules of engagement meeting or any other planning meeting, you will need to develop a process and hold a change control process meeting to obtain the group's consensus on it. You can incorporate team member process suggestions during the meeting and even use the meeting as a training in the process to help jump-start the change control process.
Can I hold a change control meeting if not all of the participants can attend?	• This is not recommended. The meeting consists of a small number of key decision-making participants and appropriate subject matter experts. They should all be present to offer their opinion about the change control so that the decision makers can make informed determinations. • If you continue to have poor attendance, attempt to find a standing meeting time that allows everyone to attend. • If the same participants fail to attend over and over, contact them off-line, reiterate the importance of their input, and attempt to uncover the root cause of their lack of participation. • If some of the subject matter experts or key decision makers are needed only for certain portions of the meeting, then formulate the agenda so participants can attend the portion of the meeting that pertains to them.
What do I do when an Issue surfaces and I discover that a risk identification meeting was never held?	• Attempt to locate any risk mitigation documentation from similar projects to provide some insight into how the issue may have been addressed in previous projects. • Whether such historical documentation exists or not, hold a crisis resolution meeting to address the immediate issue. • Hold a separate risk identification meeting as soon as possible to identify potential risks and impacts to the project.

(continued)

TABLE 8.3

Problem	Possible Solutions
There are so many meetings, both recurring and specialized, that project team participation is beginning to decline. What should I do?	• Capture learnings in your lessons learned document for future reference. • Be sure that your meeting is necessary (see Chapter Two, "When to Meet and When Not to Meet"). • Constantly evaluate the frequency, duration, and meeting objectives. • Determine if meetings need to be consolidated, extended, or shortened and review participant lists to ensure the right participants have been invited.
Not all of the closed issues and action items have been consolidated into one document. Do I really need to take the time to consolidate all the closed items before holding a turnover planning meeting?	• Yes. The closed issues list can be an invaluable tool once the effort evolves from a project to an implemented business solution. In most cases, when questions arise it's much faster to check the closed issue log and open action items than to try to locate and contact project team members who have moved on to other project efforts.

Chapter 9

Facilitating Project Close Meetings

Heaven grant that the burden you carry may have as easy
an exit as it had an entrance.
—DESIDERIUS ERASMUS, philosopher, 1466–1536

WHAT A GREAT SENSE of accomplishment for Joe and his project team! After months of initiating, planning, and striving to overcome the many barriers thrown his way, he can finally announce that the new product has been successfully implemented.

The natural high of watching all the pieces of the puzzle come together can be quite invigorating. Savor your success—that great sense of accomplishment and relief you feel the morning after (or maybe the week after) implementation. The joy gained by being part of such a cohesive team, the fatigue brought on by lack of sleep during those final hours, and, yes, the sense of sadness that something you poured so much of your professional life into are now at an end.

Working on a difficult, challenging project can be one of the most rewarding experiences of a project manager's career. Though riddled with potholes and roadblocks, the journey often stands out in your memory as being deeply satisfying. But when you were in the middle of trying to overcome those huge obstacles, which at times seemed impossible to resolve, you probably sometimes wished you were somewhere else. In fact, if you're honest with yourself, you'll probably have to admit that there were times when you never thought you'd all agree on scope, much less successfully implement or launch the effort.

Now, as you begin to look toward your next big challenge, it's time to step back and look retrospectively at all the events that led up to this point. Closing out a project, like facilitation, is as much an art as a science. You don't want to disband the project team too soon. And you don't want to hang around too long. So, when is the project *really* over? This seems like such a simple question, but it can often be difficult to answer.

No matter how successfully the project was planned and executed, if your business partners feel they were left holding the bag on unresolved issues, the effort can't be viewed as a complete success. You don't want to allow necessary handoff and closure activities to fall through the cracks. On the other hand, if you stay involved too long after the project has been implemented and after all the outstanding issues have been resolved, your business partners may begin to question your confidence in their ability to manage things going forward. Or worse, they may begin to think of you as their personal resource, which starts to blur the roles and responsibilities that were so carefully outlined in the project turnover meetings.

The end point of every project is different. So the key to a graceful exit is through a formal closing process. After all, sometimes a good exit is all you can ask for (Stewart, 2004).

Overview of the Close Phase

Closing a project is all about formally terminating the project's activities (PMI, 2004). It is assumed that those final activities will include transferring the completed product to others. However, not all projects end on a high note. Projects are canceled or fail for a number of reasons—funding is suddenly cut, resources are shifted to work on a higher-priority project, or a sudden change in the marketplace mandates an adjustment to the overall business strategy. So regardless of the reason for project termination—success or otherwise—be aware that the activities and associated meetings involved in closing a project still need to occur.

Project Close Meetings

In this chapter we'll talk about two meetings—the project wrap-up and the project retrospective meetings—that will help you make sure all the loose ends are tied up and allow you to learn and grow from your experiences. Figure 9.1 shows where these two meetings reside on the project meeting road map.

These meetings differ in purpose, audience, and intended outcome. See Table 9.1 for an overview of both of these meetings.

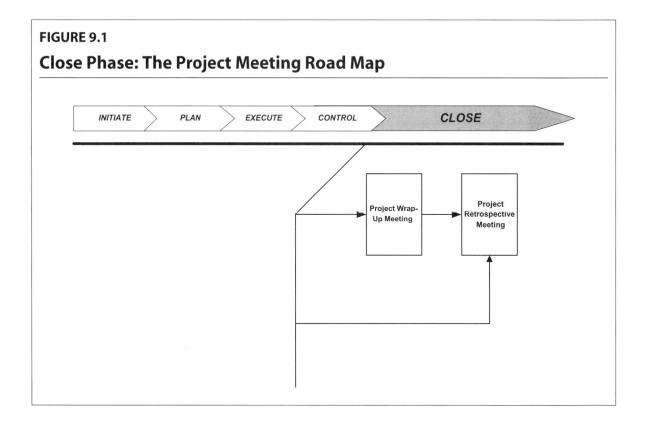

FIGURE 9.1

Close Phase: The Project Meeting Road Map

TABLE 9.1

Close Phase Project Meetings

Project Meeting	Type or Purpose	This Meeting Is Designed to	Objectives	Inputs	Outputs	Suggested Participants
Project wrap-up meeting	Information exchange	Confirm that the project is incorporated into the ongoing daily operations of the organization and tie up all the loose ends as it relates to the implementation, turnover plans, and project deliverables. This meeting should also provide feedback on the project results to goals thus far.	• To verify original scope was met as defined • To verify desired business objectives were met • To obtain buy-in and sign-off on implementation activities so that project can be officially closed • To review any outstanding or open implementation issues • To gain agreement on approach to close or resolve any open issues • To validate that all project deliverables have been finalized	• Project turnover meeting documentation • Proposed business as usual roles and responsibilities matrix • List of closed project implementation issues • List of open project implementation issues • List of project deliverables • Assessment of project results to original goals (as known at this point)	• Confirmation that original project scope and business objectives were met • Confirmation of business as usual roles and responsibilities matrix • List of open project implementation issues • Celebration party scheduled • Confirmation of completed deliverables and storage location of historical documentation	• Facilitator • Project sponsor(s) • Project manager • Product manager • Subteam owner(s) • Line of business stakeholder(s) • Marketing representative(s) • Technology representative(s) • Quality professional(s) • Testing representative(s) • Legal representative(s) • Compliance representative(s) • Subject matter expert(s)

(continued)

TABLE 9.1 *(continued)*

Project Meeting	Type or Purpose	This Meeting Is Designed to	Objectives	Inputs	Outputs	Suggested Participants
Project retrospective meeting	Creative development	Review of a consolidated list of all of the lessons learned. Evaluate which mitigation strategies worked, which did not, and why. Identify ways to incorporate learnings into future efforts.	• To share best practices • To identify processes that work well • To identify suggestions or ways to improve the process • To discuss impacts of the lesson learned (on people, process, and technology) • To identify best practices that could be applied to future efforts	• Consolidated and categorized list of all lessons learned and possible mitigation strategies • List of individual ideas and thoughts (if participants were asked to provide a sample list prior to the meeting) • Learnings that the team or individuals may want to offer from their team development or individual development meetings • List of high-level, predefined categories to spark conversation • Designation of who will own the resulting action plan	• Finalized Lessons Learned Template • List of best practices that can be applied to future efforts • Action plan for getting the improvements implemented	• Facilitator • Project management office representative(s) • Project manager • Product manager • Subteam owner(s) • Marketing representative(s) • Technology representative(s) • Quality professional(s) • Testing representative(s) • Legal representative(s) • Compliance representative(s) • Subject matter expert(s)

The Project Wrap-Up Meeting

The project wrap-up meeting is designed to confirm that the original purpose and scope of the initiative were met. To this end, it's a prime opportunity to share the progress achieved thus far toward the original project goals, so the team can see the results of their efforts (for example, we expected to have gotten fourteen thousand applications at this point and we've received twenty thousand). It also allows you to review the roles, responsibilities, and timeline outlined in the project turnover document with the larger project team. If there are any open issues or incomplete tasks on the project plan, each unresolved item must have an owner and a target due date. At the end of the project wrap-up meeting, there should be no questions about what is being transitioned from the project team to the business and when these activities will be completed.

If the project wrap-up meeting is being held because the project effort has been put on hold or canceled, the objectives differ slightly. The key objectives in those situations are to ensure that all open *and* closed issues known to date are captured and all project documentation is in proper order and ready to be stored for historical purposes.

Project Wrap-Up Meeting Participants

Determining the number of participants for the project wrap-up meeting can be quite a challenge. The number of people who want to attend these meetings tends to grow rather quickly, especially when you take into account all of the project team members who were involved. Now add to that list the number of people beginning to take over the daily operations. Keep in mind that the project wrap-up meeting is truly an information exchange meeting. The input to this meeting was created by a smaller group in the project turnover planning meetings. Again, because the number of participants can be rather substantial,

---

EXHIBIT 9.1

Managing the Time: Time-Boxing

Use time-boxing to manage information exchange meetings that have a full agenda. This technique can be especially helpful when attempting to keep a large number of participants on track and focused.

- Allow a certain amount of time to accomplish each item on the agenda.
- When an agenda item begins to extend beyond the allotted time, let the participants know that the allotted time is up.
- If the topic being discussed must be resolved in order to move forward, agree on a specific amount of time to continue discussion and adhere to it. If there's still no resolution at the end of the time allotted, record the issue and move on.
- If the topic does not need to be resolved, record the issue and move on.

---

a well-planned, time-boxed agenda and *two* project meeting facilitators can help keep the meeting focused and on track (see Exhibit 9.1).

Since a large number of folks may want to be involved in wrapping up a project—especially a successful one—consider holding it in combination with a project celebration event. This combination allows you to scale back meeting participation to include only those truly affected by and responsible for executing a smooth transition from official project to implemented business solution. Then invite the larger audience to take part in the celebration. This ensures that everyone feels involved and appreciated, yet avoids having an unwieldy number of meeting attendees. Again, when confirming your participant list, review the list of key questions found in Chapter Five (see the website for the Key Participant Checklist) to make sure you have the right participants involved.

If the project is being put on hold or canceled, you should be able to limit the number of participants to eight to twelve, as you no longer need to transition work from the project team to the line of business or operational owners.

Project Wrap-Up Meeting Inputs and Outputs

The project wrap-up meeting has two key inputs: (1) a list of all known open *and* closed issues that have been tracked throughout the life of the project and (2) the current project team and operational team roles and responsibilities (created during the project turnover planning meeting). You'll be reviewing these lists to confirm that all issues have been addressed and, if any have not, ensuring that open items are owned and scheduled for resolution by an appropriate member of the team.

Project Wrap-Up Standard Agenda

For a group of twelve or less, this meeting should take no more than two hours. But if you have more attendees, you'll need to plan for a longer meeting. It's just a fact of life—achieving a meeting goal will take longer with more people. So take that into consideration when scheduling.

The following items are most often addressed as part of this meeting:

- *Roll call.* The names of all participants and the areas they represent.
- *Thanks and acknowledgments.* Officially recognize and acknowledge all the work each individual present contributed to the project.
- *Review of project purpose and goals.* Describe how the purpose and goals were achieved by the project. This can be supported with measurements indicating progress to date.
- *Review of project deliverables.* Present a list of all the deliverables created for this project along with where they are located.
- *Review of turnover plan.* Walk through the turnover plan developed in the control phase and obtain official approval from all parties. Make changes as needed.

- *Review of open issues remaining.* Discuss each issue and get agreement on the resolution approach, owner, and anticipated date of resolution.
- *Next steps.* List anything the group should do or expect prior to the close of the project.

Project Wrap-Up: Face-to-Face or Virtual?

Although the project wrap-up meeting can be held virtually, the potential for a large number of attendees will make it challenging. So if you must hold the meeting virtually, refer to Chapter Three for suggestions on tools and techniques to keep it on target.

As mentioned previously, it is ideal when the project wrap-up meeting can be combined with a formal project celebration. By combining the two, it allows one last opportunity for all of the project team members to come together face-to-face, formally agree on the project turnover plan, and have one final event to recognize all team members for their efforts.

The Project Retrospective Meeting

The project retrospective meeting provides the opportunity to review the lessons learned throughout all phases of the project and identify which ones should be integrated into the ongoing practices of the organization. Like all other processes, the practice of project management should be regularly assessed and improved. The project retrospective meeting is one of the ways to make that happen.

Unfortunately, many organizations either allot minimal time for this meeting or dismiss it altogether. This often stems from a larger problem within the organization—there is no method for incorporating new ideas or improvements into the project management practices across the organization. If this is your situation, focus the meeting on how individuals can carry these lessons forward to their next project rather than attempting to identify changes to the organization or project methodology.

The objectives for the project retrospective meeting are to understand the lessons learned from the effort—what did the project teach us? This includes understanding how the various issues and scenarios affected the people, process, and technology involved. If the retrospective is being held because the project effort has been put on hold or canceled, the objectives remain the same. However, you'll want to include some time to reflect on what can be learned from the manner in which the project cancellation was orchestrated.

Project Retrospective Meeting Participants

The number of participants at a retrospective should be limited to no more than fifteen participants. Only those key individuals who were close to the implementation effort—such as the project manger, the subteam leaders, technology representatives, testers, and subject matter experts—should be involved.

As you plan for this meeting, remember that obtaining the right group size is a balancing act. You must balance securing the people who have the right expertise with achieving the right group size to allow you to realistically accomplish the meeting objectives.

Project Retrospective Meeting Inputs and Outputs

The key input for the retrospective meeting is a consolidated list of all of the lessons learned and best practices that have been identified and captured throughout the life of the project. This consolidated list should also include individual learnings that have been identified during the team development and individual development meetings that took place in the execute and control phases. You should go into this meeting knowing who will own and track the action plan that will result. If your organization has a project management office, they may be in the best position to encourage implementation of improvements that affect projects organization-wide (such as changes in marketing, finance, or testing that will result in faster, more successful, higher-quality project results). The retrospective meeting will result in a best practices matrix that can be used by your project management office and future project teams for continuous process improvement.

Project Retrospective Standard Agenda

At this point you may have a considerable list of items that ideally have been categorized to allow people to synthesize their thinking. But remember, your goal is not to validate each item, but to identify key lessons to incorporate into your projects going forward. For a large-scale project with numerous subteams, you might want to hold several two-hour meetings focused on specific areas of the project, such as testing, communication, or the requirements process. For a small to medium-sized project, a two-hour meeting may be sufficient. It really depends on the number of people involved and the level of detail you want to reach. We've had experiences on both ends of the spectrum, with similar results.

Here is a typical agenda for this type of meeting:

- *Roll call.* The names of all participants and the areas they represent.
- Based on the lessons listed in each category:
  - What are three things in this category we can integrate into our processes going forward to obtain better results?
  - How will each of these things become incorporated into our ongoing processes?
  - Build an action plan. It does not need to be detailed, but there should be some plan to reflect what will happen with these recommendations.

Project Retrospective: Face-to-Face or Virtual?

The project retrospective lends itself to being a virtual meeting, especially if you've gathered best practices in advance and folks have had a chance to review them. If you have several participants collocated at the same site, secure a conference room at each location and request that all participants at that site meet at the designated area. Have a projector at each site and use a web-based collaboration tool so participants at all sites can follow along visually with the discussion. This can be very effective when trying to encourage groups to collaborate and think through possible ways to integrate process improvements. It also helps eliminate the temptation to multitask, as so many people do when attending a virtual meeting by phone at their desks.

Close Phase Recurring Meetings

By the time you reach the close phase, most of the meetings that occurred during the plan and execute phases have ended. However, it's possible that two types of meetings—the project status and executive overview meetings—will continue during this phase. If held at all, these meetings will occur to address specific needs as the project enters into the close phase. One project we encountered held executive overviews well into the close phase because they couldn't decide what to do about outstanding transition issues. Another project continued holding status meetings because the team needed to finalize various project cleanup tasks. Bottom line: be flexible and realize there is no golden rule about which meetings continue into this phase. It's on a project-by-project basis.

Troubleshooting Guide

What Works and What Doesn't Work

Let's take a look at what works and what doesn't work in some of the close phase meetings. Table 9.2 offers some learnings from our experience.

TABLE 9.2

Close Phase Meetings: What Works and What Doesn't

Project Meeting	Type or Purpose	What Works	What Doesn't Work
Project wrap-up meeting	Information exchange	• Holding a face-to-face meeting and combining it with the project celebration event • Using the documentation and output from the project turnover planning meetings	• Failing to hold a wrap-up meeting in the case of a project being put on hold or canceled • Allowing the group size to become so large that no tangible output is achieved
Project retrospective meeting	Creative development	• Inviting a project management office representative to take part in discussions of how to improve project execution in the organization • Discussing how the issues and scenarios (both positive and negative) impacted the people, process, and technology involved in the implementation of the effort	• Treating this meeting as a large, final lessons learned meeting without taking the time to identify key changes to the current project organization and project methodology • Attempting to hold one large meeting to gather all participants' initial input rather than holding several smaller, more focused meetings—especially for large, complex projects • Failing to balance the necessary expertise with the appropriate group size to be productive

During the close phase of the project, here are several key things to do or to avoid doing:

- *Do* have project team members submit a list of best practices and categorize them prior to holding the project retrospective meeting.

- *Do* consider holding the project wrap-up meeting in conjunction with a project celebration event if at all possible, especially if people are coming to a location that requires travel.

- *Don't* skip the project close meetings when a project is put on hold or canceled. The activities in the close phase still need to occur.

- *Don't* let the number of participants taking part in the project turnover meeting get out of hand.

- *Don't* feel that holding a project retrospective is worthless because your company has no way of incorporating new ideas or improvements into their project management practices across the organization. Instead, focus the meeting on how individuals can carry these lessons forward to their next project.

Troubleshooting

In Table 9.3, you'll find a list of common problems that arise when facilitating meetings during the close phase and some possible solutions.

TABLE 9.3

Troubleshooting Guide for Close Phase Meetings

Problem	Possible Solutions
What do I do when my project was canceled prior to the close phase and I was reassigned to another effort?	• We suggest that you still identify the key individuals who worked on the effort, find a block of time when everyone can meet, and schedule the project wrap-up and project retrospective meetings. Even though you have a new responsibility, it is always beneficial to take the time to ensure that all the lessons learned and project deliverables (regardless of percentage complete) are accounted for and stored properly for historical purposes. You never know when the project may be resurrected, and the time spent holding these two meetings can help eliminate hours of potential repeated work that would be necessary if nothing was documented. A good rule of thumb is to ask yourself, "Would I find the historical documentation useful if I was asked to revisit this effort in a few months?"
The project team is so large that once I include all the necessary representatives from both the project team and business representatives, we will never be able to accomplish the project wrap-up meeting goals within a reasonable amount of time. What do I do?	• Logically segment the outputs from the project turnover planning meetings. Hold project wrap-up meetings with specific subteams of participants and track all of the outputs from these subteam meetings in one document. Once all of the subteam meetings have been held, send the consolidated document to the team members for their final input and comments. You may want to convene a consolidated walk-through, even if done virtually. Make the necessary updates and send the final version of the wrap-up document to team members with a due date for providing their official sign-off.
Some of the project team members were assigned to other projects immediately after the control phase. Should I still hold the project wrap-up and project retrospective meetings?	• Yes. Hold the meetings and invite all the appropriate participants. Encourage those team members already involved in other projects to attend anyway. If they can't attend, ask them to provide their insights to you prior to the meeting so that their voices can still be heard. You can develop a list of questions and send them to those participants to help focus their thoughts on the topics that will be discussed in the meeting.
The weekly project status meetings are taking longer to plan than to actually conduct at this point. Can I cancel this meeting?	• In most cases, yes. Once the project status meetings become less meaningful and the appropriate useful information is better shared by another means, then you can cancel this status meeting. • If there are still open issues being tracked with due dates assigned well into the future, change the frequency of the recurring project status meetings. If the majority of the work has been completed, you can adjust the agenda to no longer include a status update by subteam leads and refocus the time allotted to issue resolution or whatever other topic may need to be discussed.

Resources and References

Resource A

Recommended Reading

TO LEARN MORE ABOUT BASIC facilitation skills and the application of these skills to meetings and projects, we recommend the following books.

Facilitation Tools and Skills

Bens, I. *Facilitating with Ease!* San Francisco: Jossey-Bass, 2000.

Cameron, E. *Facilitation Made Easy.* London: Kogan Page, 2001.

Hunter, D., Bailey, A., and Taylor, B. *The Art of Facilitation.* Tucson, Ariz.: Fisher Books, 1995.

Hunter, D., Bailey, A., and Taylor, B. *The Zen of Groups: A Handbook for People Meeting with a Purpose.* New York: Perseus, 1995.

Jenkins, J., and Jenkins, M. *The 9 Disciplines of a Facilitator.* San Francisco: Jossey-Bass, 2006.

Justice, T., and Jamieson, D. W. *The Facilitator's Fieldbook.* New York: AMACOM/HRD Press, 1999.

Kaner, S., and others. *Facilitator's Guide to Participatory Decision-Making.* San Francisco: Jossey-Bass, 2007.

Kinlaw, D., and Roe, R. *Facilitation Skills: The ASTD Trainer's Sourcebook.* New York: McGraw-Hill, 1996.

Kiser, A. G. *Masterful Facilitation: Becoming a Catalyst for Meaningful Change.* New York: AMACOM, 1998.

Rees, F. *The Facilitator Excellence Handbook.* San Francisco: Jossey-Bass/Pfeiffer, 1998.

Schwarz, R. M. *The Skilled Facilitator.* San Francisco: Jossey-Bass, 1994.

Sibbet, D. *Principles of Facilitation: The Purpose and Potential of Leading Group Process.* San Francisco: Grove Consultants International, 2002.

Tauge, N. R. *The Quality Toolbox.* Milwaukee, Wis.: American Society for Quality/Quality Press, 1995.

Meetings

Doyle, M. *How to Make Meetings Work!* New York: Berkley Trade, 1993.

Lencioni, P. *Death by Meeting.* San Francisco: Jossey-Bass, 2004.

Mina, E. *The Business Meetings Sourcebook: A Practical Guide to Better Meetings and Shared Decision Making.* New York: AMACOM, 2002.

Mina, E. *The Complete Handbook of Business Meetings.* New York: AMACOM, 2000.

Settle-Murphy, N. *68 Tips for Getting the Most Out of Remote Meetings.* Boxborough, Mass.: Chrysalis International, 2004.

Streibel, B. *The Manager's Guide to Effective Meetings.* New York: McGraw-Hill, 2002.

Whitmore, J. *Coaching for Performance: Growing People, Performance, and Purpose.* London: Nicholas Bealey, 2002.

Wilkinson, M. *The Secrets to Masterful Meetings: Ignite a Meetings Revolution!* Atlanta, Ga.: Leadership Strategies, 2005.

Project Deliverables
Facilitating Projects

Means, J., and Adams, T. *Facilitating the Project Lifecycle.* San Francisco: Jossey-Bass, 2005.

Wood, J., and Silver, D. *Joint Application Development.* New York: Wiley, 1995.

Building Requirements

Gause, D. C., and Weinberg, G. M. *Exploring Requirements: Quality Before Design.* New York: Dorset House, 1989.

Goldsmith, R. F. *Discovering Real Business Requirements for Software Project Success.* Norwood, Mass.: Artech House, 2004.

Gottesdiener, E. *Requirements by Collaboration.* Reading, Mass.: Addison-Wesley, 2002.

Highsmith III, J. A. *Adaptive Software Development: A Collaborative Approach to Managing Complex Systems.* New York: Dorset House, 2000.

Leffingwell, D., and Widrig, D. *Managing Software Requirements: A Unified Approach.* Reading, Mass.: Addison-Wesley, 1999.

Robertson, S., and Robertson, J. *Mastering the Requirements Process.* Toronto: ACM Press, 1999.

Sommerville, I., and Sawyer, P. *Requirements Engineering: A Good Practice Guide.* New York: Wiley, 1997.

Wiegers, K. E. *Software Requirements.* (2nd ed.). Redmond, Wash.: Microsoft Press, 2003.

Defining Business Processes

Damelio, R. *The Basics of Process Mapping.* Portland, Ore.: Productivity Press, 1996.

Harmon, P. *Business Process Change: A Manager's Guide to Improving, Redesigning, and Automating Processes.* San Francisco: Morgan Kaufmann, 2002.

Jacka, J., and Keller, P. *Business Process Mapping: Improving Customer Satisfaction.* New York: Wiley, 2001.

Johann, B. *Designing Cross-Functional Business Processes.* San Francisco: Jossey-Bass, 1995.

Sharp, A., and McDermott, P. *Workflow Modeling: Tools for Process Improvement and Application Development.* Norwood, Mass.: Artech House, 2001.

Understanding Project Risk

McDermott, R. E. *The Basics of FMEA.* Portland, Ore.: Productivity Press, 1996.

Project Management

DeCarlo, D. *eXtreme Project Management*. San Francisco: Jossey-Bass, 2004.

Englund, R. L., Graham, R. J., and Dinsmore, P. C. *Creating The Project Office: A Manager's Guide to Leading Organizational Change*. San Francisco: Jossey-Bass, 2003.

Forsberg, K., Mooz, H., and Cotterman, H. *Visualizing Project Management*. New York: Wiley, 1996.

Levine, H. *Practical Project Management*. New York: Wiley, 2002.

Thomsett, R. *Radical Project Management*. Upper Saddle River, N.J.: Prentice Hall, 2002.

Wideman, R. M. *A Management Framework for Project, Program, and Portfolio Integration*. Victoria, B.C.: Trafford, 2004.

Resource B

Recommended Websites

THERE ARE MANY WEBSITES with excellent information related to meeting facilitation and projects. We recommend that you take a look at the following websites to continue your meeting facilitation journey.

Meeting Facilitation

International Association of Facilitators – www.iaf-world.org
This website provides you access to valuable facilitation resources including training organizations, facilitator certification events, publications such as the annual *Facilitation Journal* and monthly *Global Flipchart* newsletter, and the ability to "Find a Facilitator" in your area.

EffectiveMeetings.com – www.effectivemeetings.com
EffectiveMeetings.com is an online resource center designed to provide useful information about meetings in the form of articles, tips, and quizzes.

Meeting Truths – www.jkdservices.com/ims/meetingtruths
Meeting Truths is the place to come for support, advice, and expertise on all aspects of meetings. Meeting Truths is a collaborative, user-driven service, helping businesspeople across the spectrum to improve the process and results from their meetings.

Chrysalis International – www.chrysalisinternational.com
Chrysalis is a leader in the virtual meeting space. They provide workshops, webinars, articles, and guides to help those attempting to bridge the distance between team members and still remain productive.

3M Meeting Network – www.3m.com/meetingnetwork
The 3M Meeting Network provides tips on facilitating meetings and delivering presentations, offers advice and information on meeting room products, and contains a database of professional facilitators, planners, and trainers.

Meetings.Net – www.meetingsnet.com
MeetingsNet offers targeted intelligence, planning tools, and resources for meeting planners and executives.

Management by Meetings – www.managementbymeetings.com
Management by Meetings offers tools and insights to help individuals provide more effective contribution and leadership to meetings.

Group Facilitation – www.albany.edu/cpr/gf
Group Facilitation is a moderated discussion on the practice and theory of group facilitation. Participants share ideas, questions, and advice on group problem solving and decision making, group development, running meetings, and related topics. In 2006 the discussion group averaged 879 subscribers in 35 countries, with an average of 7.5 posts per day. Most participants are practicing group facilitators who work in diverse fields, such as meeting facilitation, conflict resolution, large group interventions, organization development, total quality management, electronic meeting systems, strategic planning, team building, project management, and community planning.

IAF Methods Database – www.iaf-methods.org
The IAF Methods Database is an online methods resource and knowledge-sharing community dedicated to providing

managers, team leaders, and facilitators with online and face-to-face tools for planning, leading, and following up on group meetings.

National Facilitator Database – www.nfdb.com/nfdb
This tool helps pair skilled facilitators with organizations that have facilitation needs, such as strategic planning, meeting facilitation, requirements gathering, or team building. Facilitators enter information about their skills, areas of expertise, sample clients, projects, certifications, and billing rate into a searchable database.

Project Management

4PM – Project Management – www.4pm.com
4PM.com offers project management training, certification courses, and a library of reference materials. This site includes book recommendations as well as links to articles, templates for project deliverables, tools, and descriptions of techniques.

Gantthead.com – www.gantthead.com
Gantthead.com is the online community for IT project managers. It is a resource for project professionals to find process examples, deliverable templates and samples, discussion threads, articles, and tips on the art of managing your project effort.

Max Wideman's Project Management Wisdom – www.maxwideman.com
Max Wideman is a widely acclaimed risk management expert in the project management industry; he led the development of the first PMBOK. His website is designed to provide answers to many of the questions and issues plaguing project management today.

Project Connections – www.projectconnections.com
The content of this website comes from practicing managers and team members with experience on a variety of project types—product development, IT, marketing, biotech, aerospace, and

more. It is dedicated to providing fast access to practical PM resources for those managing projects large and small who are trying to make good project management work in their organizations.

PM Forum – www.pmforum.org

The mission of the PM Forum is to use the Internet to provide an economical means for the promotion and exchange of project management information and knowledge worldwide. Its goal is to provide leaders and practitioners in project management around the world the opportunity to meet electronically, share information, and discuss issues of common global interest.

IT Toolbox Project Management Knowledge Base – http:// projectmanagement.ittoolbox.com

The IT Toolbox is a community where peers share knowledge about information technology. The Project Management Knowledge Base provides blogs, wiki's, groups, and white papers to allow interaction among IT project management professionals on topics that are important to them.

The Project Management Library – www.managementhelp .org/plan_dec/project/project.htm

This library provides easy-to-access, clutter-free, comprehensive resources on the leadership and management of projects. Content is relevant to the vast majority of people, whether they are in large or small for-profit or nonprofit organizations. Over the past ten years, the library has grown to be one of the world's largest well-organized collections of these types of resources.

Resource C

Recommended Organizations

MANY ORGANIZATIONS HAVE BEEN FORMED to promote continued learning, networking, and growth in the areas of facilitation and project management. The following list describes some organizations we've found helpful.

International Association of Facilitators (IAF) – www.iaf-world.org
The International Association of Facilitators was formed by a group of professionals desiring an avenue for interchange, professional development, trend analysis, and peer networking. Since 1994, the IAF has grown to over 1,300 members in more than twenty countries. The IAF encourages and supports the formation of local groups of facilitators to network and provide professional development opportunities for their members.

National and Regional OD Networks – www.odnetwork.org
The OD Network is dedicated to being a leader in the advancement of the theory and practice of organization development by helping to define and communicate the values, purposes, and benefits of organization development; promoting the effective and ethical use of organization development principles, tools, and best practices; supporting practitioners through

enhanced learning and professional development opportunities; providing a values-based home for OD practitioners, researchers, and educators to exchange ideas and create dialogue on critical issues; and sharing leadership and partnering with others to achieve our vision.

Project Management Institute (PMI) – www.pmi.org
PMI is a global network of over one hundred thousand project management professionals that promotes sharing of ideas and experiences through networking and project participation and provides access to industry information, seminars, and workshops on leading-edge topics.

Association of Project Management (APM) – www.apm.org.uk
APM is the largest independent professional body of its kind in Europe, with over fifteen thousand individual and four hundred corporate members throughout the United Kingdom and abroad. The aim of APM is to develop and promote project management across all sectors of industry and beyond.

The Authors

Tammy Adams, B.S., CPF, CQM, is managing partner of Chaosity LLC, which specializes in project facilitation and business process analysis. Her focus is on helping organizations simplify the chaos that exists in their business by clarifying and improving *how* they do *what* they do. Using collaborative techniques, she transforms team knowledge and experience into quality project deliverables. She is a certified professional facilitator and certified quality manager, with extensive experience in project management, operations, consulting, training, and facilitation.

Ms. Adams is a member of the editorial board of the BPM Institute and a board member for the International Association of Facilitators. She has authored several articles published in *Cutter IT Journal*, *The Facilitator*, and BPM Institute's online magazine. She is coauthor of the book *Facilitating the Project Lifecycle* and a regular speaker at international facilitator, quality, business process, and project management conferences.

Jan Means, M.S., CPF, is a principal consultant at Resource Advantage, Inc., a consulting and training firm specializing in business process innovation, organization productivity improvement, and information technology planning and design. Her experience as a senior manager, facilitator, and information systems manager and developer spans a twenty-seven-year career in a variety of industries including manufacturing, direct mail, financial services, and utilities. Her special expertise focuses on facilitation of customized work sessions, which bring business professionals together with information technology, project, and quality professionals to improve business performance. As a certified user of several psychological testing instruments, Ms. Means also works with organizations to help them understand the impact of employee preferences, behavior, and learned skills on accomplishing change and improving productivity.

She is the author of several articles about business process design and the human dynamics of change and is coauthor of the book *Facilitating the Project Lifecycle: Skills and Tools to Accelerate Progress for Project Managers, Facilitators and Six Sigma Project Teams*, published by Jossey-Bass in 2005. She is a regular speaker at international facilitator, quality, and project management conferences.

Michael S. Spivey, M.A., CPF, PMP, is a senior consultant and facilitator at Resource Advantage, Inc. Working as an operations manager, project manager, facilitator, and consultant over a twenty-year career in the financial services industry, he has a wide range of experience, from frontline management to managing enterprise-wide change initiatives. Mr. Spivey's special expertise focuses on project and program management, as well as the facilitation of work sessions that bring business and technical resources together to focus on improving overall business performance. This is accomplished through the numerous practical techniques that he models during joint business and technical work sessions. As a facilitator, he also works with organizations to transfer the knowledge of these techniques to practitioners so that they can be applied to both current and future project work.

Mr. Spivey holds a master of arts degree in human resource development from the George Washington University. He is a board member for the International Association of Facilitators (IAF), serving in the role of Professional Development Strategic Initiative coordinator. He is a certified professional facilitator (CPF), a certified assessor with the International Association of Facilitators, and a certified project management professional (PMP) with the Project Management Institute. Also, he holds Myers-Briggs Type Indicator (MBTI) certification and uses the MBTI and its principles regularly with his clients. He is a regular speaker at international facilitator, quality, and project management conferences.

References

Adams, T., and Means, J. *The Project Meeting Facilitator.* Paper presented at the ASQ Six Sigma Conference, Phoenix, Feb. 2007.

Baker, S., and Baker, K. *The Complete Idiot's Guide to Project Management.* New York: Macmillan, 1998.

Bramson, R. M. *Coping with Difficult People.* New York: Dell, 1981.

Bryce, T. "Bryce's Laws." [http://www.phmainstreet.com/mba/]. 2006. Accessed Jan. 2007.

Daly, C. *The Collaboration Handbook.* [http://www.redlodgeclearing-house.org/resources/handbook.html]. Jan. 2006, p. 1.

Duncan, M. "Effective Meeting Facilitation: The *Sine Qua Non* of Planning." [http://arts.endow.gov/resources/Lessons/Duncan1.html]. 1999. Portions of this essay first appeared as part of the National Endowment for the Arts "Lessons Learned" website [www.arts.endow.gov/resources/Lessons].

Encarta World English Dictionary (North American Edition.) Microsoft Corporation, 2006. Developed for Microsoft by Bloomsbury. "Definition of Collaboration." [http://encarta.msn.com]. Accessed Dec. 2006.

Haddad, W. (Ed.). "Is Instructional Technology a Must for Learning?" *TechKnowLogia: International Journal of Technologies for the Advancement of Knowledge and Learning*, 2003, 5 (1). [http://www.techknowlogia.org/TKL_active_pages2/CurrentArticles/t-right.asp?IssueNumber=19&FileType=HTML&ArticleID=455].

Interactive Meeting Solutions. *2004 Survey.* [http://www.Interactive MeetingSolutions.com]. Jan. 2004a.

Interactive Meeting Solutions. *2004 Survey.* [http://www.Interactive MeetingSolutions.com]. Nov. 2004b. Accessed Jan. 2007.

IT Cortex. "The Bull Survey" [http://www.it-cortex.com/Stat_Failure_Cause.htm]. 1998.

Jones, C. *Assessment and Control of Software Risks.* Upper Saddle River, N.J.: Prentice Hall, 1994.

Jones, C. *Software Assessments, Benchmarks, and Best Practices.* Boston: Addison-Wesley Longman, 2000.

Kaner, S., and others. *Facilitator's Guide to Participatory Decision-Making.* (2nd ed.). San Francisco: Jossey-Bass, 2007.

LeBoeuf, M. *Working Smart: How to Accomplish More in Half the Time.* New York: Warner Books, 1980.

Matson, E. "The Seven Sins of Deadly Meetings." *Fast Company*, 1996 (2), 123.

Means, J., and Adams, T. *Facilitating the Project Lifecycle: Skills and Tools to Accelerate Progress for Project Managers, Facilitators and Six Sigma Project Teams.* San Francisco: Jossey-Bass, 2005.

Mehrabian, A. *Nonverbal Communication.* Hawthorne, N.Y.: Walter de Gruyter, 1972.

Merriam-Webster Online Dictionary. [www.Merriam-Webster.com]. 2007.

Nixon, R. *Six Crises.* New York: Simon & Schuster, 1990.

PASS Online. "We've Got to Start Meeting Like This! A Guide to Fast, Fun and Fruitful Meetings." [http://www.passonline.com/course.aspx?course=WGSM06]. Accessed Mar. 2007.

Pierce, V., Cheesebrow, D., and Mathews Braun, L. "Facilitator Competencies." *Group Facilitation: A Research and Applications Journal*, Winter 2000, pp. 2, 27.

Prencipe, L. "Virtual Team Pointers." *InfoWorld*, July 13, 2001, p. 1. [http://www.infoworld.com/articles/ca/xml/01/07/16/010716caknow.html].

Project Management Institute. *A Guide to the Project Management Body of Knowledge: PMBOK Guide.* (3rd ed.). Newton Square, Penn.: Project Management Institute, 2004.

Resource Alliance. *Survey of Project Managers.* London: Resource Alliance, June 2006.

Ross, M. "Secrets to Successful Meetings: How to Tame Time Gobblers and Meeting Monsters." [http://www.kamaron.org/index.php/m/articles/id/6]. 2006.

Settle-Murphy, N. "Face to Face or Remote: Weighing the Pros and Cons." *Communiqué*: Chrysalis International, March 10, 2004. [http://www.chrysalisinternational.com/uploads/communique_032304.htm].

Spivey, M. "Project Meeting Evaluation Is Essential." *Resource Alliance Newsletter*, Feb. 2006.

Stewart, S. *Perfect Circle.* Northampton, Mass.: Small Beer Press, 2004.

Whitmore, J. *Coaching for Performance: Growing People, Performance, and Purpose.* London: Nicholas Brealey, 2002.

Index